The Wise and Witty
Quote Book

The Wise and Witty Quote Book

2,000 QUOTATIONS TO ENLIGHTEN, ENCOURAGE, AND ENJOY

Allen Klein

GRAMERCY BOOKS
NEW YORK

This 2005 edition is published by Gramercy Books, an imprint of Random House Value Publishing, a division of Random House, Inc., New York.

Gramercy is a registered trademark and the colophon is
a trademark of Random House, Inc.

Random House
New York • Toronto • London • Sydney • Auckland
www.randomhouse.com

Up Words for Down Days interior book design by Debra Borg

The Change-Your-Life Quote Book and *The Lift-Your-Spirits Quote Book* interior book designs by Karen Ocker

Printed and bound in the United States.

Library of Congress Cataloging-in-Publication Data
Winning words
The Wise and witty quote book : more than 2000 quotes to enlighten, encourage, and enjoy /
[edited by] Allen Klein.
p. cm.
Originally published: Winning words. New York : Portland House, 2002.
Includes index.
ISBN 0-517-22615-4
I. Quotations, English. I. Klein, Allen. II. Title.

PN6081.W493 2005
082—dc22   2005040277

10 9 8 7 6 5 4 3

For my mom,
who has often had an
up word for my down day

CONTENTS

UP WORDS FOR
DOWN DAYS

THE CHANGE-YOUR-LIFE
QUOTE BOOK

THE LIFT-YOUR-SPIRITS
QUOTE BOOK

INTRODUCTION

In the humor programs I present nationwide, I often conduct a small exercise that has a big impact. I ask the audience to read the following list of words: cheerful, fun, giggle, happy, jolly, joyful, laughing, playful, smiling.

After they finish reading the list, I ask them how they feel. Then I have them read another list. This one consists of such words as: bleak, depressed, dismal, gloom, hopeless, misery, tears, unhappy, upset. There is almost no reason to ask how they feel after reading this list. I could hear the despondency in their voices and see it in their faces.

The first list uplifted them. The second did not.

Words are simply the same twenty-six letters of the alphabet rearranged in different ways. Yet, words, and the sentences they form, are powerful tools which can either bring us down or lift us up. The quotations in this book will help you do the latter. They are all winners.

Up Words for Down Days

A quotation
at the right moment
is like bread
in a famine.

THE TALMUD

age & aging
anger & adversity

age *n*   the length of time that one has existed

ag•ing *v*   the process of growing old or maturing

Age is a question of mind over matter.
If you don't mind, it doesn't matter.
Satchel Paige

I was born in 1962. True.
And the room next to me was 1963.
Joan Rivers

I'm not interested in age.
People who tell their age are silly.
You're as old as you feel.
Elizabeth Arden

Age is not important
unless you're a cheese.
Helen Hayes

The prime of life is that fleeting time
between green and over-ripe.
Cullen Hightower

My mother always used to say:
"The older you get, the better you get,
unless you're a banana."
Rose Nylund in The Golden Girls

Wisdom doesn't automatically come with old age.
Nothing does—except wrinkles.
It's true, some wines improve with age.
But only if the grapes were good in the first place.
Abigail Van Buren

Old age isn't so bad when you consider the alternative.
Maurice Chevalier

The secret of staying young is to live honestly,
eat slowly, and lie about your age.
Lucille Ball

It's paradoxical that the idea of living a long life
appeals to everyone, but the idea of getting old
doesn't appeal to anyone.
Andy Rooney

Thirty-five is a very attractive age.
London society is full of women of the highest birth
who have, of their own free choice,
remained thirty-five for years.
Oscar Wilde

Life begins at forty.
Walter B. Pitkin

To be seventy years young is sometimes far more cheerful
and hopeful than to be forty years old.
Oliver Wendell Holmes

I've always roared with laughter when they say life begins at forty.
That's the funniest remark ever. The day I was born
was when life began for me.
Bette Davis

A woman past forty should make up her mind
to be young—not her face.
Billie Burke

Now that I'm over sixty I'm veering toward respectability.
Shelley Winters

I'm over the hill, but the climb was terrific!
Graffiti

Just remember, once you're over the hill,
you begin to pick up speed.
Charles Schulz

Old age is like a plane flying through a storm.
Once you're aboard, there's nothing you can do.
Golda Meir

The trick is growing up without growing old.
Casey Stengel

You can't help getting older,
but you don't have to get old.
George Burns

If you carry your childhood with you,
you never become older.
Abraham Sutzkever

Whatever a man's age may be,
he can reduce it several years by putting
a bright-colored flower in his buttonhole.
Mark Twain

When it comes to staying young,
a mind-lift beats a face-lift any day.
Marty Bucella

Everyone is the age of their heart.
Guatemalan saying

We are always the same age inside.
Gertrude Stein

I'll tell ya how to stay young:
Hang around with older people.
Bob Hope

Being middle-aged is a nice change from being young.
Dorothy Canfield Fisher

Middle age is when you've met so many people
that every new person you meet
reminds you of someone else.
Ogden Nash

Middle age is when your age starts to show
around your middle.
Bob Hope

Don't worry about middle age:
you'll outgrow it.
Laurence J. Peter

You know you are getting old when people tell you
how good you look.
Alan King

You know you are getting old when the candles
cost more than the cake.

Bob Hope

I smoke cigars because at my age
if I don't have something to hang onto I might fall down.

George Burns

I have everything now that I had twenty years ago—
except now it's all lower.

Gypsy Rose Lee

They tell you that you'll lose your mind when you grow
older. What they don't tell you
is that you won't miss it very much.

Malcolm Cowley

There are three signs of old age. Loss of memory...
I forget the other two.

Red Skelton

My grandfather's a little forgetful, but he likes to give me advice.
One day, he took me aside and left me there.

Ron Richards

First you forget names, then you forget faces,
then you forget to pull your zipper up,
then you forget to pull your zipper down.
Leo Rosenberg

My dad's pants kept creeping up on him.
By sixty-five he was just a pair of pants and a head.
Jeff Altman

One of the many pleasures of old age is giving things up.
Malcolm Muggeridge

I look forward to being older,
when what you look like becomes less and less an issue
and what you are is the point.
Susan Sarandon

There is many a good tune played on an old fiddle.
Old saying

There is a fountain of youth; it is your mind, your talents, the creativity
you bring to your life and the lives of the people you love. When you
will learn to tap this source, you will have truly defeated age.
Sophia Loren

I never feel age....
If you have creative work,
you don't have age or time.
Louise Nevelson

I want to tell people approaching and perhaps fearing age that it is a
time of discovery. If they say "Of what?"
I can only answer "We must find out for ourselves,
otherwise it won't be discovery."
Florida Scott-Maxwell

Anyone can get old.
All you have to do is live long enough.
Groucho Marx

How old would you be
if you didn't know how old you are?
Satchell Paige

Don't complain about growing old—
many people don't have that privilege.
Earl Warren

an•ger *n*   a strong feeling of hostility or displeasure

ad•ver•si•ty *n*   a state of hardship or distress

This makes me so sore it gets my dandruff up.
Samuel Goldwyn

The best remedy for a short temper is a long walk.
Jacqueline Schiff

Anyone can become angry. That is easy.
But to be angry with the right person, to the right degree,
at the right time, for the right purpose
and in the right way—that is not easy.
Aristotle

As a girl my temper often got out of bounds.
But one day when I became angry at a friend
over some trivial matter, my mother said to me,
"Elizabeth, anyone who angers you conquers you."
Sister Elizabeth Kenny

The greatest remedy for anger is delay.
Seneca

Grow angry slowly—there's plenty of time.
Ralph Waldo Emerson

Speak when you are angry and you will make
the best speech you will ever regret.
Ambrose Bierce

Getting angry can sometimes be like leaping into a
wonderfully responsive sports car, gunning the motor,
taking off at high speed and then discovering
the brakes are out of order.
Maggie Scarf

To rule one's anger is well; to prevent it is still better.
Tyron Edwards

If you are patient in one moment of anger,
you will escape a hundred days of sorrow.
Chinese saying

It is impossible for you to be angry and laugh at the same time.
Anger and laughter are mutually exclusive
and you have the power to choose either.
Wayne Dyer

There are two ways of meeting difficulties:
you alter the difficulties, or you alter yourself
to meet them.
Phyllis Bottome

We win half the battle when we make up our minds to take
the world as we find it, including the thorns.
Orison S. Marden

Drag your thoughts away from your troubles—by the ears,
by the heels, or any other way you can manage it.
It's the healthiest thing a body can do.
Mark Twain

When the first Superman movie came out I was
frequently asked "What is a hero?"...My answer was that a hero
is someone who commits a courageous action
without considering the consequences....Now my definition is
completely different. I think a hero is an ordinary individual who finds
strength to persevere and endure in spite of overwhelming obstacles.
Christopher Reeve

The happy and efficient people in this world are those who
accept trouble as a normal detail of human life and resolve
to capitalize it when it comes along.
H. Bertram Lewis

Problems are only opportunities in work clothes.
Henry J. Kaiser

You seek problems because you need their gifts.
Richard Bach

Everything that irritates us about others
can lead us to an understanding of ourselves. —
Carl Jung

Heartbreak is life educating us.
George Bernard Shaw

I learned long ago never to wrestle with a pig.
You get dirty, and besides, the pig likes it. —
Cyrus Ching

When things are bad, we take comfort in the thought that
they could always be worse. And when they are,
we find hope in the thought that things are so bad
they have to get better.
Malcolm Forbes

When I hear somebody sigh, "Life is hard,"
I am always tempted to ask, "Compared to what?"
Sydney J. Harris

When life's problems seem overwhelming, look around
and see what other people are coping with.
You may consider yourself fortunate.
Ann Landers

When you dig another out of their troubles,
you find a place to bury your own.
Anonymous

The human capacity to fight back will always astonish
doctors and philosophers. It seems, indeed, that there are no
circumstances so bad and no obstacles so big
that man cannot conquer them.
Jean Tetreau

The bitterest misfortune can be covered up with a smile.
Yiddish folk saying

He knows not his own strength that hath not met adversity.
Ben Jonson

Without adversity, without change, life is boring.
The paradox of comfort is that we stop trying.
John Amatt

Take chances, make mistakes. That's how you grow.
Pain nourishes your courage.
You have to fail in order to practice being brave.
Mary Tyler Moore

Although the world is full of suffering,
it is also full of the overcoming of it.
Helen Keller

You Don't Have to Suffer
Judy Tatelbaum

One of the secrets of life is to make stepping stones
out of stumbling blocks.
Jack Penn

The worst thing in your life may contain seeds of the best.
When you can see crisis as an opportunity,
your life becomes not easier, but more satisfying.
Joe Kogel

What is to give light must endure burning.
Viktor Frankl

If we had no winter, the spring would not be so pleasant.
If we did not sometimes taste of adversity,
prosperity would not be so welcome.
Anne Bradstreet

He who can't endure the bad will not live
to see the good.
Yiddish saying

The way I see it, if you want the rainbow,
you gotta put up with the rain.
Dolly Parton

If we fight against the waves that pass over us in life, we are
overpowered. If we move with the waves in life
as they roll over us, the wave passes on.
Pesikta Zurtarti

Expect trouble as an inevitable part of life
and repeat to yourself the most comforting words of all:
This, too, shall pass.
Ann Landers

change & challenge

change _v_ to cause to be different

chal•lenge _n_ a test of one's abilities in a demanding undertaking

---

It's always something.
Gilda Radner

There is nothing permanent except change.
Heraclitus

Everything is changing.
People are taking their comedians seriously
and the politicians as a joke.
Will Rogers

The more things change, the more they remain the same.
Alphonse Karr

Even if you're on the right track,
you'll get run over if you just sit there.
Will Rogers

It seems necessary to completely shed the old skin
before the new, brighter, stronger, more beautiful one
can emerge....I never thought I'd be getting
a life lesson from a snake.
Julie Ridge

Should you shield the canyons from the windstorms,
you would never see the beauty of their carvings.
Elisabeth Kübler-Ross

To keep our faces toward change and behave like free
spirits in the presence of fate is strength undefeatable.
Helen Keller

Happy is he who learns to bear what he cannot change. ✓
J. C. F. von Schiller

If matters go badly now, ✓
they will not always do so.
Horace

Perhaps one day this too will be pleasant to remember.
Virgil

This, too, shall pass. ✓
William Shakespeare

In spite of illness, in spite even of the archenemy sorrow,
one can remain alive long past the usual date
of disintegration if one is unafraid of change,
insatiable in intellectual curiosity, interested in big things,
and happy in small ways.
Edith Wharton

Changes are not only possible and predictable,
but to deny them is to be an accomplice
to one's own unnecessary vegetation.
Gail Sheehy

We cannot change anything unless we accept it.
Carl Jung

If you can't change your fate, change your attitude.
Amy Tan

A positive attitude may not solve all your problems, but it will
annoy enough people to make it worth the effort.
Herm Albright

Life is change. Growth is optional. Choose wisely. —
Karen Kaiser Clark

When you're through changing, you're through.
Bruce Barton

If you realize that all things change,
there is nothing you will try to hold onto.
Tao Te Ching

A permanent state of transition
is man's most noble condition.
Juan Ramon Jimenez

Consistency is contrary to nature, contrary to life.
The only completely consistent people are the dead.
Aldous Huxley

If you fear change, leave it here.
Sign on a restaurant tip jar

You learn more from ten days of agony ✓
than from ten years of content.
Sally Jessy Raphael

So often we try to alter circumstances to suit ourselves,
instead of letting them alter us,
which is what they are meant to do.
Mother Maribel

I have always grown from my problems and challenges,
from things that don't work out;
that's when I've really learned.
Carol Burnett

The hardships of life are sent not by an unkind
destiny to crush, but to challenge.
Sam E. Roberts

The ultimate measure of a man is not where he stands in
moments of comfort and convenience, but where he stands
at times of challenge and controversy.
Martin Luther King, Jr.

Sometimes things which at the moment may be
perceived as obstacles—and actually be obstacles,
difficulties, or drawbacks—can in the long run result
in some good end which would not have occurred
if it had not been for the obstacle.
Steve Allen

God gave burdens, also shoulders.
Yiddish saying

That which does not kill me makes me stronger.
Friedrich Nietzsche

We all have to go through the tumbler a few times
before we can emerge as a crystal.
Elisabeth Kübler Ross

The gem cannot be polished without friction,
nor man perfected without trials.
Chinese saying

Everyone gets their rough day. No one gets a free ride.
Today so far, I had a good day. I got a dial tone.
Rodney Dangerfield

I have seen what a laugh can do. It can transform almost
unbearable tears into something bearable, even hopeful.
Bob Hope

One of the things I learned the hard way was
that it doesn't pay to get discouraged. Keeping
busy and making optimism a way of life can restore
your faith in yourself.
Lucille Ball

I have never been disabled in my dreams.
Christopher Reeve

Keep your face to the sunshine
and you cannot see the shadow.
Helen Keller

The "crisis" of yesterday is the joke of tomorrow.
H. G. Wells

dating, marriage
& divorce
death & dying
diet & exercise

dat•ing *v* to go on a date with

mar•riage *n* legal union of a man and woman as husband and wife

di•vorce *n* legal dissolution of a marriage

When you're first single, you're so optimistic.
At the beginning, you're like: "I want to meet a guy who's really
smart, really sweet, really good-looking, has a really
great career."...Six months later, you're like:
"Lord—any mammal with a day job."
Carol Leifer

I was out on a date recently and the guy took
me horseback riding. That was kind of fun, until we
ran out of quarters.
Susie Loucks

Do you know the best way for a guy to impress a girl at the gym?
The best way is to do pull-ups...pull up in a Corvette, pull up in
a Rolls-Royce, pull up in a Cadillac.
Conan O'Brien

When I'm dating I look at a guy and wonder, "Is this the man I want my
children to spend their weekends with?"
Rita Rudner

Let's face it, a date is like a job interview that lasts all night. The only difference between the two is that there are very few job interviews where there's a chance you will end up naked at the end of it.

Jerry Seinfeld

Personally, I think if a woman hasn't met the right man
by the time she's 24, she may be lucky.

Deborah Kerr

A girl can wait for the right man to come along
but in the meantime that still doesn't mean she can't have
a wonderful time with all the wrong ones.

Cher

I just broke up with someone and the last thing she said to me was,
"You'll never find anyone like me again!"
I'm thinking, "I should hope not! If I don't want you,
why would I want someone like you?"

Larry Miller

My boyfriend and I broke up.
He wanted to get married and I didn't want him to.

Rita Rudner

Marriage is a great institution,
but I'm not ready for an institution yet.
Mae West

In Hollywood a marriage is a success if it outlasts milk.
Rita Rudner

Marriage is the alliance of two people,
one of whom never remembers birthdays
and the other never forgets them.
Ogden Nash

Marriage is not just spiritual communion and passionate embraces;
marriage is also three-meals-a-day
and remembering to carry out the trash.
Joyce Brothers

A successful marriage requires falling in love many times,
always with the same person.
Mignon McLaughlin

If marriage is your object,
you'd better start loving your subject.
Anonymous

All marriages are happy.
It's trying to live together afterwards
that causes all the problems.
Shelley Winters

There's only one way to have a happy marriage
and as soon as I learn what is it I'll get married again.
Clinton Eastwood

I'd marry again if I found a man who had
fifteen million dollars, would sign over half to me,
and guarantee that he'd be dead within a year.
Bette Davis

An archeologist is the best husband a woman can have;
the older she gets, the more interested he is in her.
Agatha Christie

Husbands are like fires.
They go out if unattended.
Zsa Zsa Gabor

Only two things are necessary to keep one's wife happy.
One is to let her think she is having her own way,
and the other, to let her have it.
Lyndon B. Johnson

The best way to get most husbands to do something
is to suggest that perhaps they're too old to do it.
Shirley MacLaine

The reason husbands and wives do not understand each
other is because they belong to different sexes.
Dorothy Dix

Marrying a man is like buying something you've been
admiring for a long time in a shop window.
You may love it when you get it home,
but it doesn't always go with everything else.
Jean Kerr

My parents want me to get married.
They don't care who anymore as long as he doesn't have
a pierced ear, that's all they care about. I think men who
have a pierced ear are better prepared for marriage.
They've experienced pain and bought jewelry.
Rita Rudner

I've always said we got married
because there was nothing on TV.
Bette Midler

Getting divorced just because you don't love a man
is almost as silly as getting married just because you do.
Zsa Zsa Gabor

It wasn't exactly a divorce—I was traded.
Tim Conway

I've never married, but I tell people I'm divorced
so they won't think something's wrong with me.
Elayne Boosler

Divorce: A fifty-fifty settlement of the property, where one
gets the house and the other gets the mortgage.
Evan Esar

In Hollywood, an equitable divorce settlement means
each party getting fifty percent of publicity.
Lauren Bacall

One reason people get divorced
is that they run out of gift ideas.
Robert Byrne

Being divorced is like being hit by a Mack
truck—if you survive you start looking very carefully
to the right and left.
Jean Kerr

For a while, we pondered whether
to take a vacation or get a divorce.
We decided that a trip to Bermuda is over in two weeks,
but a divorce is something you always have.
Woody Allen

That's the only good thing about divorce.
You get to sleep with your mother.
Anita Loos

death *n* termination of life

dy•ing *v* to cease living

It matters not how a man dies, but how he lives.
Samuel Johnson

The value of life lies not in the length of days,
but in the use we make of them;
a man may live long yet live very little.
Montaigne

Death is not the greatest loss in life.
The greatest loss is what dies inside us while we live.
Norman Cousins

Let us so live that when we come to die
even the undertaker will be sorry.
Mark Twain

There are worse things in life than death.
Have you ever spent an evening
with an insurance salesman?
Woody Allen

Death: Nature's way of making you slow down.
Evan Esar

Death is nature's way of saying your table is ready.
Robin Williams

✓ Death is nothing to fear. It is only another dimension.
Wayne Dyer

Death is simply a shedding of the physical body,
like the butterfly coming out of a cocoon....
It's like putting away your winter coat
when spring comes.
Elisabeth Kübler-Ross

When one man dies, one chapter is not torn out of the
book, but translated into a better language.
John Donne

One of the situations in which everybody seems to fear
loneliness is death. In tones drenched with pity,
people say of someone, "He died alone."
I have never understood this point of view.
Who wants to have to die and be polite at
the same time?
Quentin Crisp

It's not that I'm afraid to die,
I just don't want to be there when it happens.
Woody Allen

If my doctor told me I only had six minutes to live,
I wouldn't brood. I'd type a little faster.
Isaac Asimov

If you bemoan your brief stay on earth,
consider the mayfly which lives only for one day.
If the weather were bad that day,
your whole life could be rained out.
Wes "Scoop" Nisker

Everybody wants to go to heaven,
but nobody wants to die.
Joe Louis

Losing is the price we pay for living.
It is also the source of much of our growth and gain.
Judith Viorst

I think the most you can hope for at the end of life is that
your hair's messed, you're out of breath,
and you didn't throw up.
Jerry Seinfeld

We find by losing. We hold fast by letting go.
We become something new by ceasing to be something
old. This seems to be close to the heart of that mystery.
I know no more now than I ever did about the far side of
death as the last letting-go of all, but now I know that I do
not need to know, and that I do not need to be afraid of
not knowing. God knows. That is all that matters.

Frederick Buechner

To live in hearts we leave behind
Is not to die.

Thomas Campbell

The highest tribute to the dead is not grief but gratitude.

Thornton Wilder

To weep too much for the dead is to affront the living.

Old saying

Weeping may endure for a night,
but joy cometh in the morning.

Psalms 30:5

It is foolish to tear one's hair in grief,
as though sorrow would be made less by baldness.

Cicero

We learn as much from sorrow as from joy,
as much from illness as from health, from handicap as
from advantage—and indeed perhaps more.
Pearl S. Buck

If life must not be taken too seriously—
then so neither must death.
Samuel Butler

Life does not cease to be funny when people die
any more than it ceases to be serious when people laugh.
George Bernard Shaw

I mean that's what death is really, it's the last big move of
your life. The hearse is like the van, the pallbearers are
your close friends, the only ones you could really ask to
help you with a big move like that. And the casket is that
great, perfect box you've been looking for your whole life.
The only problem is once you find it, you're in it.
Jerry Seinfeld

For three days after death, hair and fingernails continue to
grow but phone calls taper off.
Johnny Carson

Of all the deathbed regrets that I have heard
not one of them has been,
"I wish I had spent more time at the office."
Wayne Dyer

Don't send me flowers when I die—give them to me now
so we can appreciate their beauty together!
C. Leslie Charles

They say such nice things about people at their funerals
that it makes me sad to realize that
I'm going to miss mine by just a few days.
Garrison Keillor

I did not attend his funeral,
but I wrote a nice letter saying I approved of it.
Mark Twain

They say you shouldn't say nothing
about the dead unless it's good.
He's dead. Good.
Moms Mabley

No matter how great a man is,
the size of his funeral usually depends on the weather.
Rosemary Clooney

No matter who you are,
you only get a little slice of the world.
Have you ever seen a hearse followed by a U Haul?
Billy Graham

The sight of a gravestone, weighty not only in its granite,
allows us perspective on problems as pressing as
burnt toast, taxes, and hay fever.
Harrowsmith Country Life

Of all escape mechanisms, death is the most efficient. ✓
H. L. Mencken

Death will be a great relief. No more interviews.
Katharine Hepburn

I can't die yet...I'm booked!
George Burns

I am ready to meet my Maker.
Whether my Maker is prepared for the ordeal
of meeting me is another matter.
Winston Churchill

I believe in sex and death—
two experiences that come once in a lifetime.
Woody Allen

The only difference between sex and death is,
with death you can do it alone and nobody's going to
make fun of you.
Woody Allen

I do not believe in an afterlife,
although I am bringing a change of underwear.
Woody Allen

Eternity is a terrible thought.
I mean, where's it going to end?
Tom Stoppard

If you die in the elevator, be sure to push the UP button.
Sam Levenson

di•et *v* to eat or drink according to a regulated system

ex•er•cise *n* activity that requires physical or mental exertion

---

One should eat to live, not live to eat.
Molière

To lengthen thy Life, lessen thy meals.
Benjamin Franklin

Never eat more than you can lift.
Miss Piggy

Food is an important part of a balanced diet.
Fran Lebowitz

I prefer Hostess fruit pies to pop-up toaster tarts
because they don't require so much cooking.
Carrie Snow

The two biggest sellers in any bookstore
are the cookbooks and the diet books.
The cookbooks tell you how to prepare the food
and the diet books tell you how not to eat any of it.
Andy Rooney

This recipe is certainly silly.
It says to separate two eggs,
but it doesn't say how far to separate them.
Gracie Allen

Artichokes...are just plain annoying....
After all the trouble you go to, you get about as much actual
"food" out of eating an artichoke as you would
from licking thirty or forty postage stamps.
Have the shrimp cocktail instead.
Miss Piggy

I'm on a seafood diet. I see food and I eat it.
Anonymous

I told my doctor I get very tired when I go on a diet, so he gave me
pep pills. Know what happened? I ate faster.
Joe E. Lewis

I've been on a diet for two weeks
and all I've lost is two weeks.
Totie Fields

I've been on a constant diet for the last two decades.
I've lost a total of 789 pounds. By all accounts, I should
be hanging from a charm bracelet.
Erma Bombeck

Eat, drink, and be merry, for tomorrow we diet!
Anonymous

I never worry about diets.
The only carrots that interest me
are the number you get in a diamond.
Mae West

To feel "fit as a fiddle," you must tone down your middle.
Anonymous

It's rough to go through life with your contents looking as if
they settled during shipping!
Milton Berle

He who does not mind his belly,
will hardly mind anything else.
Samuel Johnson

When I buy cookies I just eat four and throw the rest away. But first I spray them with Raid so I won't dig them out of the garbage later. Be careful, though, because that Raid really doesn't taste that bad.

Janette Barber

I've decided that perhaps I'm bulimic
and just keep forgetting to purge.

Paula Poundstone

I did not become a vegetarian for my health.
I did it for the health of the chickens.

Isaac Beshevis Singer

Health food makes me sick.

Calvin Trillin

Old people shouldn't eat health food.
They need all the preservatives they can get.

Robert Orben

You do live longer with bran
but you spend the last fifteen years on the toilet.

Alan King

The sovereign invigorator of the body is exercise,
and of all the exercises walking is the best.
Thomas Jefferson

A vigorous five-mile walk will do more good for an
unhappy but otherwise healthy adult than all the
medicine and psychology in the world.
Paul Dudley White

I like long walks,
especially when they are taken by people
who annoy me.
Fred Allen

My grandmother, she started walking five miles a day
when she was sixty. She's ninety-seven today—
we don't know where the hell she is.
Ellen Degeneres

You can't lose weight without exercise.
But I've got a philosophy about exercise.
I don't think you should punish your legs
for something your mouth did.
Drag your lips around the block once or twice.
Gwen Owen

The only reason I would take up jogging
is so I could hear heavy breathing again.
Erma Bombeck

I have never taken any exercise
except sleeping and resting.
Mark Twain

When I feel like exercising
I just lie down until the feeling goes away.
Robert M. Hutchins

A bear, however hard he tries,
grows tubby without exercise.
**Pooh's Little Instruction Book,
inspired by A. A. Milne**

I've been doing leg lifts faithfully for about fifteen years,
and the only thing that has gotten thinner is the carpet
where I have been doing the leg lifts.
Rita Rudner

Too many people confine their exercise to
jumping to conclusions, running up bills, stretching the truth,
bending over backward, lying down on the job,
sidestepping responsibility and pushing their luck.
Anonymous

I joined a health spa recently.
They had a sign for "Free Weights."
So I took a couple.
Scott Wood

Physical fitness is in.
I recently had a physical fit myself.
Steve Allen

friends & family

friends *n* people who one knows; acquaintances

fam•i•ly *n* a group of persons sharing common ancestry or goals

---

The only way to have a friend
is, to be one.
Ralph Waldo Emerson

A man, Sir, should keep his friendship in constant repair.
Samuel Johnson

The best way to keep your friends
is not to give them away.
Wilson Mizner

The best time to make friends is before you need them.
Ethel Barrymore

Trouble is a sieve through which
we sift our acquaintances.
Those too big to pass through are our friends.
Arlene Francis

The essence of true friendship is
to make allowances for another's little lapses.
David Storey

A friend is a person who likes you for what you are,
in spite of all your faults, all your shortcomings.
Alfred Armand Montapert

In prosperity, our friends know us;
in adversity, we know our friends.
John Churton Collins

Lots of people want to ride with you in the limo,
but what you want is someone
who will take the bus with you
when the limo breaks down.
Oprah Winfrey

A friend is someone who allows you distance
but is never far away.
Noah benShea

A true friend is someone who is there for you
when he'd rather be anywhere else.
Len Wein

True friendship is seen through the heart
not through the eyes.
Anonymous

If you are looking for a friend who has no faults,
you will have no friends.
Hasidic folk saying

Laughter is not at all a bad beginning for a friendship,
and it is far the best ending for one.
Oscar Wilde

The most valuable things in life
are not measured in monetary terms.
The really important things are not
houses and lands, stocks and bonds,
automobiles and real estate,
but friendships, trust, confidence,
empathy, mercy, love and faith.
Bertrand Russell V. Delong

The holy passion of friendship is of so sweet and steady
and loyal and enduring a nature that it will last through a
whole lifetime, if not asked to lend money.
Mark Twain

A friend costs nothing.
An enemy you must pay for.
Yiddish folk saying

A friend is a person who had the same
enemies you have.
Stephen Leacock

A friend may well be reckoned
the masterpiece of Nature.
Ralph Waldo Emerson

Friendships multiply joy and divide griefs.
H. G. Bohn

My friends are my estate.
Emily Dickinson

A faithful friend is the medicine of life.
Ecclesiastes 6:16

True friendship is like sound health,
the value of it is seldom known until it be lost.
Charles Caleb Colton

Show me a genuine case of platonic friendship,
and I shall show you two old or homely faces.
Austin O'Malley

Each friend represents a world in us,
a world possibly not born until they arrive,
and it is only by this meeting that a new world is born.
Anais Nin

Life's truest happiness is found
in friendships we make along the way.
Anonymous

The happiest business in all the world
is that of making friends,
And no investment on the street
pays larger dividends,
For life is more than stocks and bonds,
and love than rate percent,
And he who gives in friendship's name
shall reap what he has spent.
Anonymous

There are three kinds of friends:
best friends, guest friends, and pest friends.
Laurence J. Peter

Man has three friends on whose company he relies.
First, wealth which goes with him only while good fortune
lasts. Second, his relatives; they go only as far as the
grave, leave him there. The third friend, his good deeds,
go with him beyond the grave.
The Talmud

Friendship with oneself is all important, because without it
one cannot be friends with anyone else in the world.
Eleanor Roosevelt

A home-made friend wears longer
than one you buy in the market.
Austin O'Malley

Think where man's glory most begins and ends,
And say my glory was I had such friends.
William Butler Yeats

Two are better than one, for if they fall,
the one will lift up his fellow.
Ecclesiastes 4:9–10

We are each of us angels with only one wing,
and we can only fly by embracing one another.
Luciano de Crescenzo

When a friend is in trouble, don't annoy him by asking
if there is anything you can do.
Think up something appropriate and do it.
Edgar Watson Howe

But friendship is precious, not only in the shade, but in the
sunshine of life; and thanks to a benevolent arrangement
of things, the greater part of life is sunshine.
Thomas Jefferson

False friendship, like the ivy, decays and ruins
the walls it embraces; but true friendship gives new life
and animation to the object it supports.
Richard Burton

No man is useless while he has a friend.
Robert Louis Stevenson

We need old friends to help us grow old
and new friends to help us stay young.
Letty Cotton Pogrebin

In everyone's life, at some time, our inner fire goes out.
It is then burst into flame by an encounter with another
human being. We should all be thankful
for those people who rekindle the inner spirit.
Albert Schweitzer

One loyal friend is worth ten thousand relatives.
Euripides

God gives us our relatives—
thank God we can choose our friends.
Ethel Watts Mumford

The family is one of nature's masterpieces.
George Santayana

Family: A social unit where the father is concerned
with parking space, the children with outer space,
and the mother with closet space.
Evan Esar

A family is a unit composed not only of children
but of men, women, an occasional animal,
and the common cold.
Ogden Nash

If you cannot get rid of the family skeleton,
you may as well make it dance.
George Bernard Shaw

The family you come from isn't as important
as the family you're going to have.
Ring Lardner

Happiness is having a large, loving, caring, close-knit
family in another city.
George Burns

My mother loved children—
she would have given anything if I had been one.
Groucho Marx

Mother, food, love, and career,
the four major guilt groups.
Cathy Guiswite

The most remarkable thing about my mother is that for
thirty years she served the family nothing but leftovers.
The original meal has never been found.
Calvin Trillin

God could not be everywhere,
so He created mothers.
Leopold Kompert

I have found that no kisses can ever compare
to "mom" kisses, because mom kisses can heal anything.
You can have a hangnail, a broken heart, or catatonic
schizophrenia; with moms, one kiss and you're fine.
Robert G. Lee

health & healing
housekeeping

health *n*   freedom from disease or abnormality

heal•ing *v*   to restore to health

The secret of health for both mind and body
is not to mourn for the past, nor to worry about the future,
but to live the present moment wisely and earnestly.
Buddha

To be healthy, wealthy, happy and successful in any and
all areas of your life you need to be aware that you need
to think healthy, wealthy, happy and successful thoughts
twenty-four hours a day and cancel all negative,
destructive, fearful and unhappy thoughts. These two types
of thought cannot coexist if you want to share in the
abundance that surrounds us all.
Sidney Madwed

Forgiveness is the way to true health and happiness.
Gerald Jampolsky

Forgiveness is all-powerful. Forgiveness heals all ills.
Catherine Ponder

Always forgive your enemies;
nothing annoys them so much.
Oscar Wilde

The healthy, the strong individual,
is the one who asks for help when he needs it.
Whether he has an abscess on his knee or in his soul.
Rona Barrett

The best and most efficient pharmacy
is within your own system.
Robert C. Peale

You don't get ulcers from what you eat.
You get them from what's eating you.
Vicki Baum

Be careful about reading health books.
You may die of a misprint.
Mark Twain

It's no longer a question of staying healthy.
It's a question of finding a sickness you like.
Jackie Mason

He's turned his life around.
He used to be depressed and miserable.
Now he's miserable and depressed.
David Frost

I moved to New York City for my health.
I'm paranoid and New York was the only place
where my fears were justified.
Anita Weiss

When we hate our enemies, we are giving them
power over us: power over our sleep, our appetites,
our blood pressure, our health, and our happiness.
Our enemies would dance with joy if only they knew how
they were worrying us, lacerating us, and getting even
with us! Our hate is not hurting them at all, but our hate
is turning our days and nights into a hellish turmoil.
Dale Carnegie

There's a lot of people in this world
who spend so much time watching their health
that they haven't the time to enjoy it.
Josh Billings

Health is the condition of wisdom,
and the sign is cheerfulness,
—an open and noble temper.
Ralph Waldo Emerson

The simple truth is
that happy people generally don't get sick.
Bernie S. Siegel

The body is the soul's house. Shouldn't we therefore take
care of our house so that it doesn't fall into ruin?
Philo

A man too busy to take care of his health
is like a mechanic too busy to take care of his tools.
Spanish saying

If I'd known I was going to live this long,
I'd have taken better care of myself.
Jimmy Durante

Joy, temperance, and repose, Slam the door on the doctor's nose.
Henry Wadsworth Longfellow

Wondrous is the strength of cheerfulness,
and its power of endurance—
the cheerful man will do more in the same time,
will do it better, will preserve it longer,
than the sad or sullen.
Thomas Carlyle

If your capacity to acquire has outstripped your capacity
to enjoy, you are on the way to the scrap-heap.
Glen Buck

Healing in its fullest sense requires looking into our heart
and expanding our awareness of who we are.
Mitchell Gaynor

When praying for healing, ask great things of God
and expect great things from God.
But let us seek for that healing that really matters,
the healing of the heart, enabling us to trust God simply,
face God honestly, and live triumphantly.
Arlo F. Newell

Our greatest healer is sitting right under our nose,
moving in and out—our breath.
Jacquelyn Small

The greatest secret of doctors, known only to their
wives, but still hidden from the public, is that
most things get better by themselves; most things,
in fact, are better in the morning.
Lewis Thomas

The greatest healing therapy is friendship and love.
Hubert Humphrey

The mind is its own place, and in itself,
can make heaven of Hell, and a hell of Heaven.
John Milton

What your mind possesses your body expresses.
Anonymous

When an emotional injury takes place, the body begins a
process as natural as the healing of a physical wound. Let
the process happen. Trust that nature will do the healing.
Know that the pain will pass and, when it passes, you will
be stronger, happier, more sensitive and aware.
Melba Colgrove, Harold H. Bloomfield & Peter McWilliams

No day is so bad it can't be fixed with a nap.
Carrie Snow

There must be quite a few things a hot bath won't cure,
but I don't know many of them.
Sylvia Plath

The power to heal is in you,
and nonetheless there is a tendency in our culture
to project onto other people and to want them to heal us.
Andrew Weil

Never go to a doctor whose office plants have died.
Erma Bombeck

My doctor said I look like a million dollars—
green and wrinkled.
Red Skelton

Some people think that doctors and nurses
can put scrambled eggs back into the shell.
Dorothy Canfield Fisher

A rule of thumb in the matter of medical advice
is to take everything any doctor says
with a grain of aspirin.
Goodman Ace

house•keep•ing *n*   performance of household tasks

I hate housework! You make the beds, you do the dishes; and six
months later you have to start all over again.
Joan Rivers

Cleaning your house while your kids are still growing
is like shoveling the walk before it stops snowing.
Phyllis Diller

The darn trouble with cleaning the house is
it gets dirty the next day anyway, so skip a week if you have to.
The children are the most important thing.
Barbara Bush

There is no need to do any housework at all.
After the first four years the dirt doesn't get any worse.
Quentin Crisp

I would rather lie on a sofa than sweep beneath it.
Shirley Conran

The Rose Bowl is the only bowl I've ever seen
that I didn't have to clean.
Erma Bombeck

I'm a housewife. I'm not going to vacuum
'til Sears makes one you can ride on.
Roseanne

The toughest thing about being a housewife is
you have no place to stay home from.
Patricia C. Beudoin

I'm a great housekeeper.
I get divorced, I keep the house.
Zsa Zsa Gabor

Rich people do spring cleaning too.
Liz Taylor is completely exhausted after
spraying Windex on her diamonds.
Karen Lee

Thank God for dirty dishes;
they have a tale to tell.
While other folks go hungry,
we're eating pretty well.
With home, and health, and happiness,
we shouldn't want to fuss;
For by this stack of evidence,
God's very good to us.
Anonymous

There is such a build-up of crud in my oven
there is only room to bake a single cupcake.
Phyllis Diller

I can't cook. I use a smoke alarm as a timer.
Carol Siskind

I tried to save grocery money once, but some of the
suggestions were just not practical, like
"Don't shop when you're hungry,"
which eliminated all hours when the store was open.
Erma Bombeck

Be it ever so humble, there's no place like home.
John Howard Payne

A good laugh is sunshine in a house. √
William Makepeace Thackeray

kids

ba•bies *n* a very young child; an infant

chil•dren *n* a person between birth and puberty

teen•ag•ers *n* a person between ages 13 and 19

Babies are such a nice way to start people.
Don Herold

A baby is God's opinion that the world should go on.
Carl Sandburg

When you are a mother, you are never really alone
in your thoughts. A mother always has to think twice,
once for herself and once for her child.
Sophia Loren

Making the decision to have a child—it's wondrous.
It is to decide forever to have your heart
go walking around outside your body.
Elizabeth Stone

It sometimes happens, even in the best of families, that a
baby is born. This is not necessarily cause for alarm.
The important thing is to keep your wits about you
and borrow some money.

Elinor Goulding Smith

Life is a flame that is always burning itself out,
but it catches fire again every time a child is born.

George Bernard Shaw

When the first baby laughed for the first time, the laugh
broke into a thousand pieces and they all went skipping
about, and that was the beginning of fairies.

J. M. Barrie

Somewhere on this globe every ten seconds,
there is a woman giving birth to a child.
She must be found and stopped.

Sam Levenson

[On pregnancy] To me, life is tough enough
without having someone kick you from the inside.

Rita Rudner

It takes the whole village to raise the child.
African Saying

Before I got married I had six theories about bringing up
children; now I have six children and no theories.
Lord Rochester

A child is a curly, dimpled lunatic.
Ralph Waldo Emerson

Raising children is a creative endeavor,
an art, rather than a science.
Bruno Bettelheim

In automobile terms, the child supplies the power
but the parents have to do the steering.
Benjamin Spock

A child is the greatest poem ever known.
Christopher Morley

Pretty much all the honest truth telling there is in the world
is done by children.
Oliver Wendell Holmes

While we try to teach our children all about life,
our children teach us what life is all about.
Angela Schwindt

Seek the wisdom of the ages,
but look at the world through the eyes of a child.
Ron Wild

There are children playing in the streets who could solve
some of my top problems in physics, because they have
modes of sensory perception that I lost long ago.
J. Robert Oppenheimer

You don't know how much you don't know
until your children grow up and tell you
how much you don't know.
S. J. Perelman

Children ask better questions than adults.
"May I have a cookie?" "Why is the sky blue?" and
"What does a cow say?" are far more likely to elicit a
cheerful response than "Where's your manuscript?" "Why
haven't you called?" and "Who's your lawyer?"
Fran Lebowitz

Hang around doggies and kids;
they know how to play.
Geoffrey Godbey

Parents learn a lot from their children
about coping with life.
Muriel Spark

You can learn many things from children.
How much patience you have, for instance.
Franklin P. Jones

Remember, when they have a tantrum,
don't have one of your own.
Judith Kuriensky

If you listen carefully to children
you will have plenty about which to laugh.
Steve Allen

Children have more need of models than of critics.
Joseph Joubert

If I could say just one thing to parents, it would be simply
that a child needs someone who believes in him
no matter what he does.
Alice Keliher

Never fear spoiling children by making them too happy.
Happiness is the atmosphere
in which all good affections grow.
Ann Eliza Bray

The word no carries a lot more meaning when spoken by
a parent who also knows how to say yes.
Joyce Maynard

The words that a father speaks to his children in the
privacy of home are not heard by the world, but,
as in whispering-galleries, they are clearly
heard at the end and by posterity.
Jean Paul Richter

If you want children to improve, let them overhear
the nice things you say about them to others.
Haim Ginott

Most kids hear what you say;
some kids do what you say;
but all kids do what you do.
Kathleen Casey Theisa

If a child is to keep alive his inborn sense of wonder
without any such gilt from the fairies, he needs the
companionship of at least one adult who can share it,
rediscovering with him the joy, excitement and mystery of
the world we live in.
Rachel Carson

The best thing to spend on your children is your time.
Louise Hart

To help your children turn out well,
spend twice as much time with them
and half as much money.

H. Jackson Brown

Children in a family are like flowers in a bouquet;
there's always one determined to face in an opposite
direction from the way the arranger desires.

Marcelene Cox

Likely as not, the child you can do the least with
will do the most to make you proud.

Mignon McLaughlin

The way we know our kids are growing up:
The bite marks are higher.

Phyllis Diller

There are times when parenthood seems nothing but
feeding the mouth that bites you.

Peter De Vries

I take my children everywhere;
but they always seem to find their way back home.

Robert Orben

We've had bad luck with our kids—they've all grown up.

Christopher Morley

The quickest way for a parent to get a child's attention
is to sit down and look comfortable.

Lan Olinghouse

The best way to keep children home is to make the home
atmosphere pleasant—and let the air out of the tires.

Dorothy Parker

It goes without saying that you should never have
more children than you have car windows.

Erma Bombeck

Never lend your car to anyone
to whom you have given birth.

Erma Bombeck

Anyone who thinks that art of conversation is dead
ought to tell a child to go to bed.

Robert Gallagher

Any kid will run an errand for you,
if you ask him at bedtime.

Red Skelton

I have found the best way to give advice
to your children is to find out what they want
and then advise them to do it.

Harry S Truman

The easiest way to convince my kids that they don't really
need something is to get it for them.
Joan Collins

Grandchildren are God's way
of compensating us for growing old.
Mary H. Waldrip

Be nice to your kids. They choose your nursing home.
Bumper sticker

Adolescence is like cactus.
Anais Nin

Adolescence is that period in kids' lives
when their parents become more difficult.
Ryan O' Neal

There's nothing wrong with teenagers
that reasoning with them won't aggravate.
Anonymous

The teenagers ain't all bad. I love 'em if nobody else does.
There ain't nothin' wrong with young people.
Jus' quit lyin' to 'em.
Moms Mabley

Teenagers travel in droves, packs swarms....
To the librarian, they're a gaggle of geese.
To the cook, they're a scourge of locusts.
To department stores they're a big beautiful
exaltation of larks...
all lovely and loose and jingly.
Bernice Fitz-Gibbon

Remember that as a teenager you are at the last stage
in your life when you will be happy to hear
that the phone is for you.
Fran Lebowitz

Teenagers are hormones with feet.
Marsha Doble

life & living

life *n*   the state or condition of a living organism

liv•ing *n*   the condition or action of maintaining life

Life is all memory, except for the one present moment
that goes by you so quickly you hardly catch it going.
Tennessee Williams

Life isn't a matter of milestones, but of moments.
Rose Kennedy

I am beginning to learn that it is the sweet, simple things
of life which are the real ones after all.
Laura Ingalls Wilder

Sooner or later we all discover that the important moments
in life are not the advertised ones, not the birthdays, the
graduations, the weddings, not the great goals achieved.
The real milestones are less prepossessing. They come to
the door of memory unannounced, stray dogs that amble
in, sniff around a bit, and simply never leave.
Our lives are measured by these.
Susan B. Anthony

If I had my life to live over again...I would have
more actual troubles and less imaginary ones.
Oh, I've had my moments, and if I had to do it over
again, I'd have more of them. In fact, I'd try to have
nothing else, just moments, one after another.

Nadine Stair

If I had to live my life again,
I'd make the same mistakes, only sooner.

Tallulah Bankhead

If I had my life to live over,
I'd live over a delicatessen.

Anonymous

Life is like a box of chocolates.

Forrest Gump

Life is too short to stuff a mushroom.

Shirley Conran

Life is better than death, I believe, if only because
it is less boring, and because it has fresh peaches in it.

Alice Walker

Life is far too important a thing
ever to talk seriously about.

Oscar Wilde

Not a shred of evidence exists in favor of the idea
that life is serious.
Brendan Gill

Life is too tragic for sadness.
Let us rejoice.
Edward Abbey

In every moment, the quality of your life is on the line.
In each, you are either fully alive or relatively dead.
Dan Millman

Life is no brief candle to me. It is a sort of
splendid torch which I've got hold of for the moment
and I want to make it burn as brightly as possible
before handing it on to the future generations.
George Bernard Shaw

Life is not so bad if you have plenty of luck,
a good physique and not too much imagination.
Christopher Isherwood

Life is like a ten-speed bike.
Most of us have gears we never use.
Charles Schulz

Life is a great big canvas;
throw all the paint on it you can.
Danny Kaye

Life is like a blanket too short. You pull it up and
your toes rebel, you yank it down and shivers meander
about your shoulder; but cheerful folks manage to draw
their knees up and pass a very comfortable night.
Marion Howard

I am convinced that life is 10% what happens to me
and 90% how I react to it.
Charles Swindoll

Life is not the way it's supposed to be. It's the way it is.
The way you cope with it is what makes the difference.
Virginia Satir

Remember, life is not what happens to you
but what you make of what happens to you.
Everyone dies, but not everyone fully lives.
Too many people are having "near-life experiences."
Anonymous

I think of life itself, now, as a wonderful play
that I've written for myself....And so my purpose is
to have the most fun playing my part.
Shirley MacLaine

If you're too busy to enjoy life, you're too busy.
Jeff Davidson

Do not take life too seriously.
You will never get out of it alive.
Elbert Hubbard

All I can say about life is, Oh God, enjoy it!
Bob Newhart

Life is a jest; and all things show it.
I thought so once; but now I know it.
John Gay

Be glad of life because it gives you the chance to love,
and to work, and to play and to look up at the stars.
Henry Van Dyke

One should sympathize with the joy, the beauty, the color
of life—the less said about life's sores the better.
Oscar Wilde

So much sadness exists in the world
that we are all under obligation to contribute
as much joy as lies within our powers.
John Sutherland Bonnell

It's a funny thing about life;
if you refuse to accept anything but the best,
you very often get it.
W. Somerset Maugham

The happiness of your life depends
upon the quality of your thoughts.
Marcus Antonius

The greatest discovery of any generation is that human
beings can alter their lives by altering their attitudes.
Albert Schweitzer

I realized that if what we call human nature can be
changed, then absolutely anything is possible.
From that moment, my life changed.
Shirley MacLaine

The grand essentials to happiness in this life
are something to do, something to love
and something to hope for.
Joseph Addison

We act as though comfort and luxury were the chief
requirements of life, when all that we need to make us
really happy is something to be enthusiastic about.
Charles Kingsley

Life is a paradise for those who love
many things with a passion.
Leo Buscaglia

The secret of life is to have a task,
something you devote your entire life to,
something you bring everything to, ever minute of the day
for the rest of your life. And the most important thing is,
it must be something you cannot possibly do.
Henry Moore

I have very strong feelings about how you lead your life.
You always look ahead, you never look back.
Ann Richards

Living in the past is a dull and lonely business;
looking back strains the neck muscles,
causes you to bump into people not going your way.
Edna Ferber

Life is like playing a violin solo in public,
and learning the instrument as one goes on.
Samuel Butler

Life can only be understood backwards;
but it must be lived forwards.
Søren Kierkegaard

Nobody gets to live life backward.
Look ahead—that's where your future lies.
Ann Landers

The best way to prepare for life is to begin to live.
Elbert Hubbard

If you want my final opinion on the mystery
of life and all that, I can give it to you in
a nutshell. The universe is like a safe
to which there is a combination.
But the combination is locked up in the safe.
Peter De Vries

Life is the greatest of all bargains; you get it for nothing.
Yiddish saying

Life is something to do when you can't get to sleep.
Fran Lebowitz

Life would be infinitely happier if we could only be born at
the age of eighty and gradually approach eighteen.
Mark Twain

Life:
Another game that is played with cards:
post-, greeting, punch, and credit.
Evan Esar

The purpose of life is a life of purpose.
Robert Byrne

We make a living by what we get,
but we make a life by what we give.
Winston Churchill

Only a life lived for others is a life worthwhile.
Albert Einstein

When people are serving, life is no longer meaningless.
John Gardner

There must be more to life than having everything!
Maurice Sendak

The best advice I ever received was from a friend, who
once told me, "You can have anything you want.
You just can't have everything you want."
John-Roger & Peter McWilliams

The best advice I've ever received? How about the strangest?
When I was thirteen, my father took me aside and told me that all
a girl needed to know to get by in life was written on the top of a
mayonnaise jar. I puzzled for days about the meaning of the phrase,
"Refrigerate After Opening"—until my father remarked that in his day
mayo jars always said, "Keep Cool, Don't Freeze."
C. E. Crimmins

In three words I can sum up everything
I've learned about life. It goes on.
Robert Frost

Enjoy the little things in life, for one day you may look
back and realize they were the big things.
Anonymous

One of the secrets of a happy life
is continuous small treats.
Iris Murdoch

My advice to you is not to inquire why or whither,
but just enjoy your ice cream while it's on your plate.
Thornton Wilder

There are two things to aim at in life:
first, to get what you want; and, after that, to enjoy it.
Only the wisest of mankind achieve the second.
Logan Pearsall Smith

I finally figured out the only reason
to be alive is to enjoy it.
Rita Mae Brown

I don't want to get to the end of my life
and find that I lived just the length of it.
I want to have lived the width of it as well.
Diane Ackerman

Every day we should hear at least one little song,
read one good poem, see one exquisite picture, and,
if possible, speak a few sensible words.
Johann Wolfgang von Goethe

Don't be afraid to go out on a limb.
That's where the fruit is.
H. Jackson Brown

Life engenders life. Energy creates energy.
It is by spending oneself that one becomes rich.
Sarah Bernhardt

Look, I really don't want to wax philosophic, but
I will say that if you're alive, you got to flap your arms
and legs, you got to jump around a lot, you got to make a
lot of noise, because life is the very opposite of death.
And therefore, as I see it, if you're quiet, you're not living.
You've got to be noisy, or at least your thoughts should be
noisy and colorful and lively.
Mel Brooks

Live as if you expected to live a hundred years,
but might die tomorrow.
Ann Lee

Beginning today, treat everyone you meet
as if they were going to be dead by midnight.
Extend to them all the care, kindness and
understanding you can muster, and do with no thought
of any reward. Your life will never be the same again.
Og Mandino

There are two ways of spreading light:
to be the candle or the mirror that reflects it.
Edith Wharton

Most of the shadows of this life are caused by
our standing in our own sunshine.
Ralph Waldo Emerson

The world is a mirror: what looks in looks out.
It gives back only what you lend it.
Ludwig Boeme

The follies which a person regrets most in his life are those
he didn't commit when he had the opportunity.
Helen Rowland

Twenty years from now you will be more disappointed
by the things you didn't do than by the ones you did.
So throw off the bowlines. Sail away from the safe
harbor. Catch the trade winds in your sails.
Explore. Dream. Discover.

Mark Twain

First I was dying to finish high school and start college.
And then I was dying to finish college and start working.
And then I was dying to marry and have children
to grow old enough so I could return to work.
And then I was dying to retire. And now, I am dying...
and suddenly realize I forgot to live.

Anonymous

Live in such a way that you would not be ashamed to sell
your parrot to the town gossip.

Will Rogers

There are only two ways to live your life.
One is as though nothing is a miracle.
The other is as though everything is a miracle.

Albert Einstein

It's all a miracle.
I have adopted the technique of living life
from miracle to miracle.

Arthur Rubinstein

If we could see the miracle of a single flower clearly,
our whole life would change.
Buddha

The art of being happy lies in the power of
extracting happiness from common things.
Henry Ward Beecher

Anyone can be happy when times are good;
the richer experience is to be happy when times are not.
Susan Harris

All the wonderful things in life are so simple that one is not
aware of their wonder until they are beyond touch.
Frances Gunther

Lightness of touch and living in the moment are
intertwined. One cannot dance well unless one is
completely in time with the music,
not leaning back to the last step
or pressing forward to the next one,
but poised directly on the present step as it comes.
Anne Morrow Lindbergh

The moment you know how, you begin to die a little.
The artist never entirely knows. We guess. We may be wrong,
but we take leap after leap in the dark.
Agnes de Mille

We are not permitted to choose the frame of our destiny.
But what we put into it is ours.
Dag Hammarskjöld

You don't get to choose how you're going to die. Or when.
You can only decide how you're going to live. Now.
Joan Baez

Your only obligation in any lifetime is
to be true to yourself.
Richard Bach

Other people attempt to live their lives backwards;
they try to have more things or more money, in order
to do more of what they want, so they will be happier.
The way it actually works is the reverse. You must first
be who you really are, then do what you need to do,
in order to have what you want.
Margaret Mead

Think of all the beauty still left around you and be happy.
Anne Frank

There is nothing worse than being born
extraordinarily beautiful, nothing more potentially
damaging to the self. You could say the same for being
born inordinately rich. You suddenly realize how wise the idea is that
you get nothing at birth except things to transcend. That's all you get.

Milton Glaser

I didn't belong as a kid, and that always bothered me.
If only I'd known that one day my differentness
would be an asset, then my early life
would have been much easier.

Bette Midler

He who has the why to live
can bear with almost any how.

Friedrich Nietzsche

You are the creature of circumstance or the creator.

Cavett Robert

Getting born is like being given a ticket to the theatrical
event called life. It's like going to the theater. Now, all that
ticket will get you, is through the door. It doesn't get you a good time
and it doesn't get you a bad time. You go in and sit down and you
either love the show or you don't. If you do, terrific. And if you don't—
That's show business.

Stewart Emery

Don't wait around for other people to be happy for you. Any happiness you get you've got to make yourself.
Alice Walker

The last of human freedoms—to choose one's attitude in any given set of circumstances, to choose one's own way.
Victor Frankl

If you can spend a perfectly useless afternoon in a perfectly useless manner, you have learned how to live.
Lin Yutang

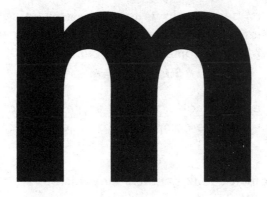

men & women
money matters

men *n* adult male human beings

wom•en *n* adult female human beings

What is most beautiful in virile men is something feminine;
what is most beautiful in feminine women
is something masculine.
Susan Sontag

The ideal man has the strength of a male
and the compassion of a female.
Zohar

Women speak because they wish to speak,
whereas a man speaks only when driven to speech
by something outside himself—
like for instance, he can't find any clean socks.
Jean Kerr

Every man who is high up likes to think he has done it all
himself; and the wife smiles, and lets it go at that.
It's our only joke. Every woman knows that.
J. M. Barrie

It's not the men in my life, but the life in my men.
Mae West

I never hated a man enough to give him diamonds back.
Zsa Zsa Gabor

If men can run the world, why can't they stop
wearing neckties? How intelligent is it to start the day
by tying a little noose around your neck?
Linda Ellerbee

Why are women wearing perfumes that smell
like flowers? Men don't like flowers. I've been
wearing a great scent.
It's called New Car Interior.
Rita Rudner

Give a man a fish and he has food for a day;
teach him how to fish and you can get rid of him
for the entire weekend.
Zenna Schaffer

Men aren't men until they can get to Sears by themselves.
Tim Allen

If a woman gets nervous, she'll eat or go shopping.
A man will attack a country—
it's a whole other way of thinking.
Elayne Boosler

Fighting is essentially a masculine idea;
a woman's weapon is her tongue.
Hermione Gingold

When men reach their sixties and retire, they go to pieces.
Women go right on cooking.
Gail Sheehy

Remember, Ginger Rogers did everything Fred Astaire did,
but she did it backwards and in high heels.
Faith Whittlesey

I hate women because
they always know where things are.
James Thurber

The people I'm furious with are the Women's Liberationists.
They keep getting up on soapboxes and proclaiming
women are brighter than men. That's true, but it should be
kept quiet or it ruins the whole racket.
Anita Loos

We women don't care too much about getting our pictures
on money as long as we can get our hands on it.
Ivy (Maude) Baker Priest

There's really nothing wrong with a woman welcoming all men's advances, darling, as long as they are in cash.
Zsa Zsa Gabor

I bank at a women's bank.
It's closed three or four days a month due to cramps.
Judy Carter

The trouble with some women is they get all excited about nothing—and then they marry him.
Cher

Women complain about sex more often than men.
Their gripes fall into two major categories:
(1) Not enough (2) Too much.
Ann Landers

Why does a woman work ten years to change a man's habits and then complain that he's not the man she married?
Barbra Streisand

The only time a woman really succeeds in changing a man is when he's a baby.
Natalie Wood

Show me a woman who doesn't feel guilty
and I'll show you a man.
Erica Jong

Sometimes I wonder if men and women really suit each other. Perhaps
they should live next door and just visit now and then.
Katharine Hepburn

Men and women, women and men. It will never work.
Erica Jong

mon•ey *n* official currency issued by a government

Money is better than poverty if only for financial reasons.
Woody Allen

Money is a good thing to have.
It frees you from doing things you dislike.
Since I dislike doing nearly everything, money is handy.
Groucho Marx

Money is relative...the more money that rolls in
the more the relatives.
Anonymous

Money talks all right. Usually it says, "Good-bye."
Anonymous

On income tax day I am reminded that while people say
money talks, mine seems to go without saying a word.
Mary Ellen Pinkham

I'm proud to pay taxes in the United States;
the only thing is, I could be just as proud
for half the money.
Arthur Godfrey

I believe we should all pay our tax bill with a smile.
I tried—but they wanted cash.
Anonymous

It is more blessed to give than to receive.
Acts 20:35

Not only is it more blessed to give than receive—
it is also deductible.
Anonymous

Money doesn't always bring happiness.
People with ten million dollars are no happier
than people with nine million dollars.
Hobart Brown

There's no reason to be the richest man in the cemetery.
You can't do any business from there.
Colonel Sanders

I didn't want to be rich.
I just wanted enough to get the couch reupholstered.
Kate (Mrs. Zero) Mostel

If you want to know how rich you really are,
find out what would be left of you tomorrow
if you should lose every dollar you own tonight.
W. J. Boetcker

Measure wealth not by the things you have,
but by the things you have for which
you would not take money.
Anonymous

The man is the richest whose pleasures are the cheapest.
Henry David Thoreau

The richest man in the world is not the one
who still has the first dollar he ever earned.
It's the man who still has his best friend.
Martha Mason

If you want an accounting of your worth,
count your friends.
Merry Browne

What's money?
A man is a success if he gets up in the morning
and goes to bed at night and in-between
does what he wants to do.
Bob Dylan

To fulfill a dream, to be allowed to sweat over lonely labor,
to be given a chance to create, is the meat and potatoes
of life. The money is gravy.
Bette Davis

Not he who has much is rich, but he who gives much.
Erich Fromm

None are so poor that they have nothing to give...
and none are so rich that they have nothing to receive.
Pope John Paul II

There is enough in the world for everyone's need,
but not enough for everyone's greed.
Frank Buchman

Money is like water. When water is moving
and flowing, it cleanses, it purifies, it makes things green,
it's beautiful. But when it starts to slow down and sludge,
it becomes toxic and stagnant.
Lynne Twist

Money is like manure. If you spread it around
it does a lot of good, but if you pile it up in one place
it stinks like hell.
Clint Murchison

Money is just a fertilizer. It can feed
nightmares or dreams.
Sharon Riddell

When starting out, don't worry about not having
enough money. Limited funds are a blessing,
not a curse. Nothing encourages creative thinking
in quite the same way.
H. Jackson Brown

I thank fate for having made me born poor. Poverty taught
me the true value of the gifts useful to life.
Anatole France

A poor person who is unhappy is in a better position than
a rich person who is unhappy. Because the poor person has hope.
He thinks money would help.
Jean Kerr

Put not your trust in money, but put your money in trust.
Oliver Wendell Holmes

A lot of people will urge you to put some money in a bank,
and in fact—within reason—this is very good advice. But don't go
overboard. Remember, what you are doing is giving your money
to someone else to hold on to, and I think that it is worth keeping
in mind that the businessmen who run banks are so worried about
holding on to things that they put little chains on all their pens.
Miss Piggy

I don't have a savings account
because I don't know my mother's maiden name.
Paula Poundstone

Never invest your money in anything
that eats or needs repairing.
Billy Rose

Invest in yourself, your family, your friends, your planet,
if you want a HIGH return.
Sharon Riddell

Invest in inflation. It's the only thing going up.
Will Rogers

The safest way to double your money is to fold it over
once and put it in your pocket.
Kin Hubbard

Money can't buy love—
but it certainly puts you in a wonderful
bargaining position.
Harrison Baker

Money can't buy friends,
but you can get a better class of enemy.
Spike Milligan

Money won't buy happiness, but it will pay the salaries
of a large research staff to study the problem.
Bill Vaughan

I see no point in money except to buy off anxiety.
I don't want to be rich. I want to be unanxious.
Sir John Betjeman

Money is good for bribing yourself through
the inconveniences of life.
Gottfried Reinhardt

The most popular labor-saving device is still money.
Phyllis George

If you want money, ask for money.
"I am enjoying the large sums of money that flow into my life,
quickly and effortlessly, this or something better for my highest good
and the highest good of all concerned."
John-Roger & Peter McWilliams

Why is there always so much month left
at the end of the money?
Anonymous

I couldn't be out of money. I still have checks.
Attributed to Gracie Allen

The most beautiful words in the English language are "Check Enclosed."
Dorothy Parker

It's good to have money and the things
that money can buy; but it's good, too, to
check up once in a while and make sure that
you haven't lost the things that money can't buy.
George Horace Lorimer

Certainly there are lots of things in life
that money won't buy, but it's very funny—
Have you ever tried to buy them without money?
Ogden Nash

I can't take it with me I know
But will it last until I go?
Martha F. Newmeyer

Yesterday is a canceled check;
tomorrow is a promissory note;
today is the only cash you have.
Spend it wisely.
Anonymous

pain & pleasure

pain *n* suffering or distress

plea•sure *n* feeling of being pleased or gratified

Never a lip is curved with pain
That can't be kissed into smiles again.
Bret Harte

The trick is not how much pain you feel—
but how much joy you feel.
Any idiot can feel pain.
Life is full of excuses to feel pain,
excuses not to live,
excuses, excuses, excuses.
Erica Jong

Simply put, you believe that things
or people make you unhappy,
but this is not accurate.
You make yourself unhappy.
Wayne Dyer

What marks the artist
is his power to shape the material of pain we all have.
Lionel Trilling

You will not grow if you sit
in a beautiful flower garden,
but you will grow if you are sick,
in pain, experience losses,
and if you do not put your head in the sand,
but take the pain and learn to accept it,
not as a curse or punishment
but as a gift to you
with a very, very specific purpose.
Elisabeth Kübler-Ross

Pain is important;
how we evade it, how we succumb to it,
how we deal with it, how we transcend it.
Audre Lorde

Those who have suffered understand suffering
and therefore extend their hand.
Patti Smith

I don't think of all the misery
but the beauty that still remains.
Anne Frank

We tire of those pleasures we take,
but never of those we give.
John Petit-Senn

Pleasure: An agreeable feeling
caused by getting the last laugh, having the last word,
or paying the last installment.
Evan Esar

Pleasure is the only thing to live for.
Nothing ages like happiness.
Oscar Wilde

Why not seize the pleasure at once?
How often is happiness destroyed by preparation,
foolish preparation!
Jane Austen

The great pleasure in life is
doing what people say you cannot do.
Walter Bagehot

You find yourself refreshed in the presence of
cheerful people. Why not make an honest effort
to confer that pleasure on others?
Half the battle is gained if you never allow
yourself to say anything gloomy.
Lydia M. Child

One of the most lasting pleasures you can experience
is the feeling that comes over you when you genuinely
forgive an enemy—whether he knows it or not.
O. A. Battista

Think big thoughts but relish small pleasures.
H. Jackson Brown Jr.

S

stress & burnout
success & failure

stress *n* an upsetting condition caused by adverse external influences

burn•out *n* physical or emotional exhaustion

The chief cause of stress is reality.
Lily Tomlin

No one can escape stress, but you can learn
to cope with it. Practice positive thinking...
seize control in small ways.
Adele Scheele

I read this article. It said the typical symptoms
of stress are eating too much, smoking too much,
impulse buying and driving too fast.
Are they kidding? This is my idea of a great day!
Monica Piper

Stress is the resistance to what's happening right now.
As we allow ourselves to open to this moment fully,
there is absolutely no stress.
Stephan Rechtschaffen

Stress is basically a disconnection from the earth,
a forgetting of the breath. Stress is an ignorant state.
It believes that everything is an emergency.
Nothing is that important. Just lie down.
Natalie Goldberg

Keep breathing.
Sophie Tucker

Stress—that confusion created when the mind must
override the body's basic desire to choke the living #*?!@
out of some idiot who desperately needs it.
Office sign

Nothing is more destined to create deep-seated anxieties
in people than the false assumption that
life should be free from anxieties.
Archbishop Fulton J. Sheen

If I knew what I was so anxious about,
I wouldn't be so anxious.
Mignon McLaughlin

Nothing erases unpleasant thoughts more effectively
than conscious concentration on pleasant ones.
Hans Selye

If you can't help it, don't think about it.
Carmel Myers

For fast acting relief, try slowing down.
Lily Tomlin

suc•cess   *n*   the achievement of something desired

fail•ure   *n*   not achieving the desired end

Success is never a destination—it's a journey.
Satenig St. Marie

Success is that old A B C—ability, breaks, and courage.
Charles Luckman

Success is simply a matter of luck. Ask any failure.
Earl Wilson

Success is often achieved by those
who don't know that failure is inevitable.
Coco Chanel

Success to me is having ten honeydew melons
and eating only the top half of each one.
Barbra Streisand

Success has gone to my hips.
Dolly Parton

Life is a series of moments,
to live each one is to succeed.
Corita Kent

There is only one success—
to be able to spend your life in your own way.
Christopher Morley

Success has nothing to do with what you gain in life or
accomplish for yourself. It's what you do for others.
Danny Thomas

I must admit that I personally measure success
in terms of the contributions an individual makes
to her or his fellow human beings.
Margaret Mead

A true measure of your worth includes
all the benefits others have gained from your success.
Cullen Hightower

Success isn't measured by the position you reach in life;
it's measured by the obstacles you overcome.
Booker T. Washington

I owe my success to having listened respectfully
to the very best advice, and then going away
and doing the exact opposite.
G. K. Chesterton

If I wanted to become a tramp, I would seek information and advice from the most successful tramp I could find. If I wanted to become a failure, I would seek advice from men who have never succeeded. If I wanted to succeed in all things, I would look around me for those who are succeeding, and do as they have done.
Joseph Marshall Wade

Decide what you want, decide what you are willing to exchange for it. Establish your priorities and go to work.
H. L. Hunt

Be like a postage stamp—
stick to one thing till you get there.
Josh Billings

You can have anything you want if you want it desperately enough. You must want it with an inner exuberance that erupts through the skin and joins the energy that created the world.
Sheila Graham

To be successful, the first thing to do is
fall in love with your work.
Sister Mary Lauretta

If you don't do it excellently, don't do it at all.
Because if it's not excellent, it won't be profitable or fun,
and if you're not in business for fun or profit,
what the hell are you doing there?
Robert Townsend

What I wanted was to be allowed to do the thing
in the world that I did best—which I believed then
and believe now is the greatest privilege there is.
When I did that success found me.
Debbi Fields

Make no little plans; they have no magic to stir men's
blood....Make big plans, aim high in hope and work.
Daniel H. Burnham

Don't be afraid to take a big step if one is indicated.
You can't cross a chasm in two small jumps.
David Lloyd George

You can have big plans,
but it's the small choices that have the greatest power.
They draw us toward the future we want to create.
Robert Cooper

Far better it is to dare mighty things,
to win glorious triumphs even though
checkered by failures, than to rank with those
poor spirits who neither enjoy nor suffer much
because they live in the gray twilight
that knows neither victory nor defeat.
Theodore Roosevelt

Victory is won not in miles but in inches. Win a little now,
hold your ground, and later, win a little more.
Louis L'Amour

Shoot for the moon.
Even if you miss it you will land among the stars.
Les Brown

Some succeed because they are destined to;
most succeed because they are determined to.
Anatole France

When I thought I couldn't go on, I forced myself to keep
going. My success is based on persistence, not luck.
Estee Lauder

Nothing in the world can take the place of persistence.
Talent will not; Genius will not; Education will not;
Persistence and determination alone are omnipotent.
Calvin Coolidge

On the secret to success: Early to bed, early to rise, work like hell, and advertise.
Gertrude Boyle

The only place you find success before work is in the dictionary.
May V. Smith

If at first you don't succeed you're running about average.
M. H. Alderson

Success is getting what you want; happiness is wanting what you get.
Anonymous

That man is a success who has lived well, laughed often and loved much.
Robert Louis Stevenson

Let no feeling of discouragement prey upon you, and in the end you are sure to succeed.
Abraham Lincoln

There is but one secret to success—never give up!
Ben Nighthorse Campbell

To laugh often and much, to win the respect
of intelligent people and the affection of children;
to earn the appreciation of honest critics and endure
the betrayal of false friends; to appreciate beauty;
to find the best in others; to leave the world a bit better,
whether by a healthy child, a garden patch
or a redeemed social condition; to know even one life has
breathed easier because you have lived.
This is to have succeeded.
Ralph Waldo Emerson

Success is a state of mind.
If you want success, start thinking of yourself as a success.
Joyce Brothers

If you have made mistakes...there is always another
chance for you...you may have a fresh start any moment
you choose, for this thing we call "failure" is not
the falling down, but the staying down.
Mary Pickford

Only those who dare to fail greatly
can ever achieve greatly.
Robert Kennedy

Our greatest glory is not in never failing,
but in rising up every time we fail.
Ralph Waldo Emerson

Fall seven times, stand up eight.
Japanese saying

For every failure, there's an alternative
course of action. You just have to find it.
When you come to a roadblock, take a detour.
Mary Kay Ash

Failure is the opportunity
to begin again more intelligently.
Henry Ford

There is much to be said for failure.
It is more interesting than success.
Max Beerbohm

To lose
Is to learn.
Anonymous

Failure is success if we learn from it.
Malcolm Forbes

Don't think of it as failure.
Think of it as time-released success.
Robert Orben

There is no failure except in no longer trying.
Elbert Hubbard

You may be disappointed if you fail,
but you are doomed if you don't try.
Beverly Sills

Never let the fear of striking out get in your way.
Babe Ruth

Do not be afraid of defeat. You are never so near to
victory as when defeated in a good cause.
Henry Ward Beecher

Remember that a kick in the ass is a step forward.
Anonymous

Act as though it were impossible to fail.
Dorothea Brande

Keep your eye on your heroes, not on your zeroes.
Robert H. Schuller

I don't know the key to success,
but the key to failure is trying to please everybody.
Bill Cosby

Quit now, you'll never make it.
If you disregard this advice, you'll be halfway there.
David Zucker

If at first you don't succeed,
do it the way your wife told you to.
Yvonne Knepper

To those who need encouragement, remember this:
Beware of quitting too soon. Dr. Seuss' first children's
book was rejected by 23 publishers.
The 24th publisher sold 6 million copies.
Ann Landers

time & technology
travel troubles

time *n*   an interval separating two points of a continuum

tech•nol•o•gy *n*   the scientific method used to achieve an
objective

Nothing is ours except time.
Seneca

Counting time is not so important as making time count.
James J. Walker

Time:
Nature's way of preventing everything
from happening at once.
Evan Esar

You lose a lot of time hating people.
Marian Anderson

One always has time enough, if one will apply it well.
Johann Wolfgang von Goethe

The time you enjoy wasting is not wasted time.
Bertrand Russell

Nothing puzzles me more than time and space;
and yet nothing troubles me less,
as I never think about them.
Charles Lamb

I never think of the future. It comes soon enough.
Albert Einstein

Time wounds all heels.
Bennett Cerf

I would I could stand on a busy corner, hat in hand, and
beg people to throw me all their wasted hours.
Bernard Berenson

If it weren't for Philo T. Farnsworth, inventor of television,
we'd still be eating frozen radio dinners.
Johnny Carson

If it weren't for electricity
we'd all be watching television by candlelight.
George Gobel

Computers are useless. They can only give you answers.
Pablo Picasso

Television enables you to be entertained in your home
by people you wouldn't have in your home.
David Frost

Thanks to television, for the first time the young are seeing
history made before it is censored by their elders.
Margaret Mead

I find television very educational. Every time someone turns
on the set I go into the other room and read a book.
Groucho Marx

Television has proved that people will look at anything
rather than each other.
Ann Landers

There is no reason anyone would want
a computer in their home.
Ken Olson, founder of Digital Equipment Corp., 1977

I think there is a world market for maybe five computers.
Thomas Watson, Chairman of IBM, 1943

Computers in the future may weigh
no more than 1.5 tons.
Popular Mechanics, 1949

Computers make it easy to do a lot of things,
but most of the things they make it easier to do,
don't need to be done.
Andy Rooney

To err is human, but to really foul things up
requires a computer.
Anonymous

This telephone has too many shortcomings
to be seriously considered as a means of communication.
The device is inherently of no value to us.
Western Union internal memo, 1876

Fax machine:
A device that allows someone in another state
to pile work on your desk.
Mrs. Webster's Guide to Business

One machine can do the work of fifty ordinary men.
No machine can do the work of one extraordinary man.
Elbert Hubbard

trav•el *v* to go from one place to another

The journey, not the arrival, matters;
the voyage, not the landing.
Paul Theroux

It is good to have an end to journey towards;
but it is the journey that matters, in the end.
Ursula K. LeGuin

To travel hopefully is a better thing than to arrive.
Robert Louis Stevenson

Ride the horse in the direction that it's going.
Werner Erhard

It isn't how much time you spend somewhere that makes it
memorable; it's how you spend the time.
David Brenner

The really happy man
is one who can enjoy the scenery on a detour.
Anonymous

Humor is the traveler's first line of defense.
Travel without humor is like sex without love.
You can do it, but what's the point really?
Mary Morris

The scientific theory I like best is that the rings of Saturn
are composed entirely of lost airline luggage.
Mark Russell

He who would travel happily must travel light.
Antoine de Saint-Exupéry

I never travel without my diary.
One should always have something sensational to read.
Oscar Wilde

It is easier to find a traveling companion
than to get rid of one.
Art Buchwald

Never play peek-a-boo with a child on a long plane trip.
There's no end to the game.
Finally I grabbed him by the bib and said,
"Look, it's always gonna be me!"
Rita Rudner

A wise man travels to discover himself.
James Russell Lowell

Though we travel the world over to find the beautiful,
we must carry it with us or we find it not.
Ralph Waldo Emerson

Keep things on your trip in perspective, and you'll be
amazed at the perspective you'll gain on things back
home while you're away....One's little world is put into
perspective by the bigger world out there.
Gail Rubin Bereny

A man travels the world over in search of what he needs
and returns home to find it.
George Moore

work weary
worrywarts

work *n*   effort directed toward the accomplishment of something

---

I never did a day's work in my life.
It was all fun.
Thomas Edison

Nothing is really work
unless you would rather be doing something else.
J. M. Barrie

In the long run you will receive more from life
doing the job you enjoy than you will ever earn
in money from a job you loathe.
Terry L. Mayfield

Do What You Love, the Money Will Follow
Marsha Sinetar

The secret of joy in work
is contained in one word—excellence.
To know how to do something well is to enjoy it.
Pearl S. Buck

The supreme accomplishment is
to blur the line between work and play.
Arthur Toynbee

It is amazing how much people can get done
if they do not worry about who gets the credit.
Sandra Swinney

Anyone can do any amount of work,
provided it isn't the work
he is supposed to be doing at that moment.
Robert Benchley

I long to accomplish a great and noble task,
but it is my chief duty to accomplish small tasks
as if they were great and noble.
Helen Keller

All labor that uplifts humanity has dignity and importance
and should be undertaken with painstaking excellence.
Martin Luther King, Jr.

Every morning I get up and look through
the Forbes list of the richest people in America.
If I'm not there, I go to work.
Robert Orben

I don't have anything against work.
I just figure, why deprive somebody who really loves it?
Dobie Gillis

Work is what you do so that some time
you won't have to do it anymore.
Alfred Polgar

Hard work never killed anybody,
but why take a chance?
Charlie McCarthy (Edgar Bergen)

If you have a job without aggravations,
you don't have a job.
Malcolm Forbes

The highest reward for a man's toil
is not what he gets for it
but what he becomes by it.
John Ruskin

√ What makes you worthwhile is who you are,
not what you do.
Marianne Williams

Generate so much loving energy that people want
to just come and hang out with you.
And when they show up, bill them!
Stuart Wilde

Occasionally indulging in a do-nothing day
is more than worth the price.
Malcolm Forbes

wor•ry *v* to feel concerned or uneasy about something

Don't worry. Be happy.
Meher Baba

Worry a little every day
and in a lifetime you will lose a couple of years.
If something is wrong, fix it if you can.
But train yourself not to worry.
Worry never fixes anything.
Mary Hemingway

There is no good in arguing with the inevitable.
The only argument with an east wind
is to put on your overcoat.
James Russell Lowell

Worry does not empty tomorrow of its sorrow,
it empties today of its joy.
Anonymous

Don't waste the years struggling for things
that are unimportant. Don't destroy your peace of mind
by looking back, worrying about the past.
Live in the present, enjoy the present.
Henry David Thoreau

You're only here for a short visit.
Don't hurry, don't worry.
And be sure to smell the flowers along the way.
Walter Hagen

If you keep on saying things are going to be bad,
you have a good chance of being a prophet.
Isaac Bashevis Singer

Money is another pressure.
I'm not complaining,
I'm just saying that there's a certain luxury
in having no money. I spent ten years in New York
not having it, not worrying about it.
Suddenly you have it, then you worry,
where is it going?
Am I doing the right thing with it?
Dustin Hoffman

You cannot prevent the birds of sorrow
from flying over your head,
but you can prevent them
from building nests in your hair.
Chinese saying

Walk away from it until you're stronger.
All your problems will be there when you get back,
but you'll be better able to cope.
Lady Bird Johnson

When I look back on all the worries
I remember the story of the old man
who said on his deathbed
that he had had a lot of trouble in his life,
most of which never happened.
Winston Churchill

What we anticipate seldom occurs;
what we least expected generally happens.
Benjamin Disraeli

Worry often gives a small thing a big shadow.
Swedish saying

Worry is interest paid on trouble before it falls due.
Dean Inge

The game is supposed to be fun.
If you have a bad day, don't worry about it.
You can't expect to get a hit every game.
Yogi Berra

Most of my major disappointments
have turned out to be blessings in disguise.
So whenever anything bad does happen to me,
I kind of sit back and feel, well,
if I give this enough time,
it'll turn out that this was good,
so I shan't worry about it too much.
William Gaines

Even in the deepest sinking there is the hidden purpose of
an ultimate rising. Thus it is for all men, from none is the
source of light withheld unless he himself withdraws from it.
Therefore the most important thing is not to despair.
Hasidic saying

My advice to actresses is don't worry about your looks.
The very thing that makes you unhappy in your
apprearance may be the one thing to make you a star.
Estelle Winwood

You'll have a better day if you think about where you're going than what's stuck to the bottom of your shoes.
Tammy Hansen Gilbert

There are two days about which nobody should ever worry, and these are yesterday and tomorrow.
Robert J. Burdette

What me worry?
Alfred E. Neuman

The
Change-Your-Life
Quote Book

To change one's life:
Start immediately.
Do it flamboyantly.
No exceptions.
WILLIAM JAMES

Actions speak
louder than words

Alter your attitude

Saying is one thing and doing is another.

MONTAIGNE

What you do speaks so loudly that I cannot hear what you say.

RALPH WALDO EMERSON

Speak little, do much.

BENJAMIN FRANKLIN

**We know what a person thinks not when he
tells us what he thinks, but by his actions.**

ISAAC BASHEVIS SINGER

Things won are done, joy's soul lies in the doing.

WILLIAM SHAKESPEARE

**Get all the education you can, but then, by God, do
something. Don't just stand there; make it happen.**

LEE IOCOCCA

**Perhaps the most valuable result of all education is the
ability to make yourself do the thing you have to do,
when it ought to be done, whether you like it or not.**

WALTER BAGEHOT

The truth of the matter is that you always know
the right thing to do. The hard part is doing it.

H. NORMAN SCHWARZKOPF

They talk most who have the least to say.

MATTHEW PRIOR

There are very few people who don't become
more interesting when they stop talking.

MARY LOWRY

Noise proves nothing—often a hen who has merely
laid an egg, cackles as if she had laid an asteroid.

MARK TWAIN

The superior man is modest in his speech,
but exceeds in his actions.

CONFUCIUS

The people who get on in this world are the people
who get up and look for the circumstances they
want, and, if they can't find them, make them.

GEORGE BERNARD SHAW

There are two kinds of people: those who don't do what they want to do, so they write down in a diary about what they haven't done, and those who haven't time to write about it because they're out doing it.

RICHARD FLOURNOY AND LEWIS R. FOSTER

If you have something to do that is worthwhile doing, don't talk about it ... do it.

GEORGE W. BIOUNT

Action is the antidote to despair.

JOAN BAEZ

Activity and sadness are incompatible.

CHRISTIAN BOVEE

Action may not always bring happiness; but there is no happiness without action.

BENJAMIN DISRAELI

All the beautiful sentiments in the world weigh less than a single lovely action.

JAMES RUSSELL LOWELL

Words are mere bubbles of water,
but deeds are drops of gold.

CHINESE PROVERB

Let every action aim solely at the common good.

MARCUS AURELIUS

...the moment one definitely commits
oneself, then Providence moves too.

GOETHE

It is better to light one candle than to curse the darkness.

CHRISTOPHER SOCIETY, MOTTO

Change your thoughts and you change your world.

NORMAN VINCENT PEALE

The most powerful thing you can do to change the
world, is to change your own beliefs about the nature
of life, people, reality, to something more positive.

SHAKTI GAWAIN

Watch your thoughts; they become words.
Watch your words; they become actions.
Watch your actions; they become habits.
Watch your habits; they become character.
Watch your character; it becomes your destiny.

FRANK OUTLAW

If you think you can do a thing or
think you can't do a thing, you're right.

HENRY FORD

In the province of the mind, what one believes
to be true either is true or becomes true.

JOHN LILLY

If you want to reach a goal, you must "see the reaching"
in your own mind before you actually arrive at your goal.

ZIG ZIGLAR

The mind is its own place, and in itself, can
make heaven of Hell, and a hell of Heaven.

JOHN MILTON

The last of the human freedoms—to choose one's attitude
in any given set of circumstances, to choose one's own way.

VIKTOR FRANKL

We cannot choose the things that will happen to us. But we can choose the attitude we will take toward anything that happens. Success or failure depends on your attitude.

ALFRED A. MONTAPERT

Seek out that particular mental attribute which makes you feel most deeply and vitally alive, along with which comes the inner voice which says, "This is the real me," and when you have found that attitude, follow it.

WILLIAM JAMES

The greatest revolution of our generation is the discovery that human beings, by changing the inner attitudes of their minds can change the outer aspects of their lives.

WILLIAM JAMES

Even a thought, even a possibility can shatter us and transform us.

FRIEDRICH NIETZSCHE

Two men look out through the same bars; one sees the mud and one the stars.

FREDERICK LANGBRIDGE

The greatest part of our happiness or misery depends on our dispositions and not on our circumstances.

MARTHA WASHINGTON

The meaning of things lies not in the things
themselves but in our attitude towards them.

ANTOINE DE SAINT-EXUPÉRY

Most people are searching for happiness. They're looking
for it. They're trying to find it in someone or something outside
of themselves. That's a fundamental mistake. Happiness is
something that you are, and it comes from the way you think.

WAYNE DYER

A happy person is not a person in a certain set of circumstances,
but rather a person with a certain set of attitudes.

HUGH DOWNS

Remember happiness doesn't depend upon who you are
or what you have; it depends solely upon what you think.

DALE CARNEGIE

Ultimately . . . it's not the stories that determine our
choices, but the stories that we continue to choose.

SYLVIA BOORSTEIN

I keep the telephone of my mind open to peace, harmony, health, love
and abundance. Then, whenever doubts, anxiety, or fear try to call me,
they keep getting a busy signal—and soon they'll forget my number.

EDITH ARMSTRONG

Be Grateful

Believe in Miracles

God gave you a gift of 86,400 seconds today.
Have you used one to say "thank you"?

WILLIAM ARTHUR WARD

Take one thing with another, and the world is a pretty good sort
of a world, and it is our duty to make the best of it, and be thankful.

BENJAMIN FRANKLIN

Feeling gratitude and not expressing it
is like wrapping a present and not giving it.

WILLIAM ARTHUR WARD

Gratitude is not only the greatest of virtues,
but the parent of all the others.

CICERO

If the only prayer you say in your whole
life is "Thank you," that would suffice.

MEISTER ECKHART

He who receives a benefit with gratitude
repays the first installment on his debt.

SENECA

Appreciation is like an insurance policy.
It has to be renewed every now and then.

DAVE MCINTYRE

Birds sing after a storm; why shouldn't people feel
as free to delight in whatever remains to them?

ROSE FITZGERALD KENNEDY

Sunshine is delicious, rain is refreshing, wind braces us up,
snow is exhilarating; there is really no such thing as
bad weather, only different kinds of good weather.

JOHN RUSKIN

Not being beautiful was the true blessing . . .
Not being beautiful forced me to develop my inner
resources. The pretty girl has a handicap to overcome.

GOLDA MEIR

'Tis better to have loved and lost than never to have loved at all.

ALFRED, LORD TENNYSON

To be upset over what you don't have is to waste what you do have.

KEN KEYES, JR.

Health is . . . a blessing that money cannot buy.

IZAAK WALTON

√ **Think of the ills from which you are exempt.**

JOSEPH JOUBERT

Count your blessings, not your crosses,
Count your gains, not your losses.
Count your joys instead of your woes,
Count your friends instead of your foes.
Count your health, not your wealth.

OLD PROVERB

He who limps still walks.

STANISLAW LEC

Too many people miss the silver lining
because they're expecting gold.

MAURICE SETTER

If you count all your assets,
you always show a profit.

ROBERT QUILLEN

A piece of the miracle process
has been reserved for each of us.

JIM ROHN

Where there is great love there are miracles.

WILLA CATHER

The world is full of wonders and miracles
but man takes his little hand and covers
his eyes and sees nothing.

ISRAEL BAAL SHEM

Miracles happen to those who believe in them.

BERNARD BERENSON

In any project the important factor is your belief.
Without belief there can be no successful outcome.

WILLIAM JAMES

The thing always happens that you really believe in;
and the belief in a thing makes it happen.

FRANK LLOYD WRIGHT

The only way to live is to accept each minute as an unrepeatable
miracle, which is exactly what it is: a miracle and unrepeatable.

STORM JAMESON

There are only two ways to live your life.
One is as though nothing is a miracle. The
other is as though everything is a miracle.

ALBERT EINSTEIN

Everything is miraculous. It is miraculous
that one does not melt in one's bath.

PABLO PICASSO

To be alive, to be able to see, to walk . . . it's all a miracle. I have
adapted the technique of living life from miracle to miracle.

ARTHUR RUBINSTEIN

All the things of the universe are perfect
miracles, each as profound as any.

WALT WHITMAN

That greatest miracle of all, the human being.

MARYA MANNES

There is a giant asleep within every man.
When that giant awakes, miracles happen.

FREDERICK FAUST

Miracles, in the sense of phenomena we cannot explain,
surround us on ever hand: life itself is the miracle of miracles.

GEORGE BERNARD SHAW

We couldn't conceive of a miracle if none had ever happened.

LIBBIE FUDIM

Expect a miracle!

ORAL ROBERTS

Cultivate

Kindness & Compassion

No one cares how much you know,
until they know how much you care.

DON SWARTZ

Kindness is the language which
the deaf can hear and the blind can see.

MARK TWAIN

One kind word can warm three winter months.

JAPANESE PROVERB

Kind words can be short and easy to
speak but their echoes are truly endless.

MOTHER TERESA

Kindness is a hard thing to give away;
it keeps coming back to the giver.

RALPH SCOTT

Kindness is never wasted. If it has no effect on
the recipient, at least it benefits the bestower.

S. H. SIMMONS

You have it easily in your power to increase the sum total of
this world's happiness now. How? By giving a few words of
sincere appreciation to someone who is lonely or discouraged.
Perhaps you will forget tomorrow the kind words you say
today, but the recipient may cherish them over a lifetime.

DALE CARNEGIE

I expect to pass through life but once. If therefore,
there be any kindness I can show, or any good thing I can
do to any fellow being, let me do it now, and not defer
or neglect it, as I shall not pass this way again.

WILLIAM PENN

Life is not so short but that there is
always time enough for courtesy.

RALPH WALDO EMERSON

A pat on the back, though only a few vertebrae removed
from a kick in the pants, is miles ahead in results.

BENNETT CERF

If you step on people in this life
you're going to come back as a cockroach.

WILLIE DAVIS

Until you have learned to be tolerant with those who do not
always agree with you; until you have cultivated the habit of
saying some kind word of those whom you do not admire;
until you have formed the habit of looking for the good instead of
the bad there is in others, you will be neither successful nor happy.

NAPOLEAN HILL

Keep in mind that the true meaning of an individual is how
he treats a person who can do him absolutely no good.

ANN LANDERS

Be nice to people on your way up because
you'll meet them on your way down.

WILSON MIZNER

Never look down on anybody unless you're helping them up.

JESSE JACKSON

The individual is capable of both great compassion
and great indifference. He has it within his means to
nourish the former and outgrow the latter.

NORMAN COUSINS

When a man has compassion for others,
God has compassion for him.

TALMUD

Compassion for yourself translates into
compassion for others.

SUKI JAY MUNSELL

It's only in our minds that we are
separate from the rest of the world.

GAY LUCE

Until he extends the circle of his compassion to all
living things, man will not himself find peace.

ALBERT SCHWEITZER

I think the purpose of life is to be useful, to be responsible,
to be honorable, to be compassionate. It is, after all, to matter:
to count, to stand for something, to have made some
difference that you lived at all.

LEO ROSTEN

Often the most loving thing we can do when a friend is
in pain is to share the pain—to be there even when we have
nothing to offer except our presence and even when being
there is painful to ourselves.

M. SCOTT PECK

Shall we make a new rule of life from tonight:
always to try to be a little kinder than is necessary?

J. M. BARRIE

That old law about "an eye for an eye" leaves everybody blind.

MARTIN LUTHER KING, JR.

Dream

the impossible dream

"One *can't* believe impossible things." "I daresay you
haven't had much practice," said the Queen. "When I was your
age, I always did it for half-an-hour a day. Why, sometimes
I've believed as many as six impossible things before breakfast."

LEWIS CARROLL

It is difficult to say what is impossible, for the dream of
yesterday is the hope of today and the reality of tomorrow.

ROBERT H. GODDARD

All big things in this world are done by people who are
naive and have an idea that is obviously impossible.

FRANK RICHARDS

Man is so made that whenever anything fires his soul,
impossibilities vanish.

LA FONTAINE

A dream is in the mind of the believer, and in
the hands of the doer. You are not given a dream,
without being given the power to make it come true.

ANONYMOUS

Don't be afraid of the space between your dreams
and reality. If you can dream it, you can make it so.

BELVA DAVIS

If one advances confidently in the direction of his dreams, and endeavors to live the life which he has imagined, he will meet with a success unexpected in common hours.

HENRY DAVID THOREAU

If you have enough fantasies, you're ready, in the event that something happens.

SHEILA BALLANTYNE

Hitch your wagon to a star.

RALPH WALDO EMERSON

Reach high, for stars lie hidden in your soul. Dream deep, for every dream precedes the goal.

PAMELA VAULL STARR

Follow your bliss.

JOSEPH CAMPBELL

My parents taught me that I could do anything I wanted and I have always believed it to be true. Add a clear idea of what inspires you, dedicate your energies to its pursuit and there is no knowing what you can achieve, particularly if others are inspired by your dream and offer their help.

PETE GOSS

To live on purpose, follow your heart and live your dreams.

MARCIA WIEDER

Within your heart, keep one still, secret spot where dreams may go.

LOUISE DRISCOLL

The future belongs to those who believe in the beauty of their dreams.

ELEANOR ROOSEVELT

All our dreams can come true—if we have
the courage to pursue them.

WALT DISNEY

Far away there in the sunshine are my highest
aspirations. I may not reach them but I can look up and
see their beauty, believe in them and try to follow them.

LOUISA MAY ALCOTT

Everything starts as somebody's daydream.

LARRY NIVEN

Dreams are extremely important.
You can't do it unless you imagine it.

GEORGE LUCAS

You see things; and you say "Why?" But I dream
things that never were; and I say "Why not?"

GEORGE BERNARD SHAW

The Wright brothers flew right through the smoke screen of impossibility.

CHARLES F. KETTERING

There comes a time in a man's life when to get where he has to
go—if there are no doors or windows—he walks through a wall.

BERNARD MALAMUD

Believe in something larger than yourself.

BARBARA BUSH

As long as you're going to think anyway, think big.

DONALD TRUMP

Doctors and scientists said that breaking the four-minute mile was
impossible, that one would die in the attempt. Thus, when I got up
from the track after collapsing at the finish line, I figured I was dead.

ROGER BANNISTER

Always listen to experts. They'll tell you
what can't be done and why. Then do it.

ROBERT HEINLEIN

The ark was built by amateurs and the
Titanic by experts. Don't wait for experts.

MURRAY COHEN

I owe my success to having listened respectfully to the very
best advice, and then going away and doing the exact opposite.

G. K. CHESTERTON

Most people never run far enough on their first wind, to find
out if they've got a second. Give your dreams all you've got
and you'll be amazed at the energy that comes out of you.

WILLIAM JAMES

Why not go out on a limb? Isn't that where the fruit is?

FRANK SCULLY

Whatever you can do, or dream you can—begin
it. Boldness has genius, power, and magic in it.

GOETHE

There are no rules of architecture for a castle in the clouds.

G. K. CHESTERTON

If you have built castles in the air, your work need not be lost; that
is where they should be. Now put the foundations under them.

HENRY DAVID THOREAU

Embrace Change

Enjoy Today

To exist is to change, to change is to mature,
to mature is to go on creating oneself endlessly.

HENRI BERGSON

Even if you're on the right track, you'll get run over if you just sit there.

WILL ROGERS

One must never lose time in vainly regretting the
past or in complaining against the changes which cause us
discomfort, for change is the essence of life.

ANATOLE FRANCE

We must change in order to survive.

PEARL BAILEY

When you're through changing, you're through.

BRUCE BARTON

Since we live in a changing universe, why do men oppose
change?... If a rock is in the way, the root of a tree will change
its direction. The dumbest animals try to adapt themselves to changed
conditions. Even a rat will change its tactics to get a piece of cheese.

MELVIN B. TOLSON

Change is a challenge and an opportunity, not a threat.

PRINCE PHILLIP OF ENGLAND

Change is often rejuvenating, invigorating, fun ... and necessary.

LYNN POVICH

The first step toward change is acceptance ... Change is
not something you do, it's something you allow.

WILL GARCIA

All changes, even the most longed for, have their melancholy,
for what we leave behind us is a part of ourselves;
we must die to one life before we can enter into another.

ANATOLE FRANCE

Each new season grows from the leftovers from the past.
That is the essence of change, and change is the basic law.

HAL BORLAND

Everything is connected ... no one thing can change by itself.

PAUL HAWKEN

Be the change that you want to see in the world.

MAHATMA GANDHI

If you don't like the way the world is, you
change it. You have an obligation to change it.

MARIAN WRIGHT EDELMAN

Will you be the rock that redirects the course of the river?

CLAIRE NUER

The world will not change until we do.

JIM WALLIS

When we are no longer able to change a
situation . . . we are challenged to change ourselves.

VIKTOR FRANKL

Never underestimate your power to change yourself:
never overestimate your power to change others.

H. JACKSON BROWN, JR.

Things don't change. You change your way of looking, that's all.

CARLOS CASTANEDA

Everything flows, nothing stays still.

HERACLITUS

Be Here Now

RAM DASS

And if not now, when?

TALMUD

Life is a great and wondrous mystery, and the only thing we know
that we have for sure is what is right here right now. Don't miss it.

LEO BUSCAGLIA

Yesterday is a canceled check; tomorrow is a promissory
note; today is the only cash you have—so spend it wisely.

KAY LYONS

How we spend our days is, of course, how we spend our lives.

ANNIE DILLARD

The only history that is worth a tinker's
damn is the history we make today.

HENRY FORD

I have everything I need to enjoy my here and now—unless
I am letting my consciousness be dominated by demands and
expectations based on the dead past or the imagined future.

KEN KEYES, JR.

You can clutch the past so tightly to your chest that
it leaves your arms too full to embrace the present.

JAN GLIDEWELL

He who lives in the present lives in eternity.

LUDWIG WITTGENSTEIN

Tomorrow's life is too late. Live today.

MARCUS VALERIUS MARTIAL

Today is the first day of the rest of your life.

CHARLES DEDERICH

It's not that "today is the first day of the rest of
my life," but that now is all there is of my life.

HUGH PRATHER

Yesterday is ashes; tomorrow wood.
Only today does the fire burn brightly.

ESKIMO SAYING

The past is a bucket of ashes, so live not in your yesterdays,
nor just for tomorrow, but in the here and now.

CARL SANDBURG

The past cannot be regained, although we can learn
from it; the future is not yet ours even though we
must plan for it . . . Time is now. We have only today.

CHARLES HUMMELL

This is the day which the Lord has made.
Let us rejoice and be glad in it.

PSALMS 118:24

This day is all that is good and fair. It is too dear, with its
hopes and invitations, to waste a moment on the yesterdays.

RALPH WALDO EMERSON

There are two days in the week about which and upon
which I never worry... One of these days is Yesterday...
And the other day I do not worry about is Tomorrow.

ROBERT JONES BURDETTE

I live now and only now, and I will do what I want to do this
moment and not what I decided was best for me yesterday.

HUGH PRATHER

I have learned to live each day as it comes, and not to
borrow trouble by dreading tomorrow. It is the
dark menace of the future that makes cowards of us.

DOROTHY DIX

We know nothing of tomorrow; our
business is to be good and happy today.

SYDNEY SMITH

You don't save a pitcher for tomorrow. Tomorrow it may rain.

LEO DUROCHER

Don't put off for tomorrow what you can do today,
because if you enjoy it today you can do it again tomorrow.

JAMES A. MICHENER

Some people are making such thorough preparation for
rainy days that they aren't enjoying today's sunshine.

WILLIAM FEATHER

So never let a cloudy day ruin your sunshine, for
even if you can't see it, the sunshine is still there,
inside of you ready to shine when you will let it.

AMY PITZELE

If you let yourself be absorbed completely, if you surrender completely
to the moments as they pass, you live more richly those moments.

ANNE MORROW LINDBERGH

I can feel guilty about the past, apprehensive about the future,
but only in the present can I act. The ability to be in the
present moment is a major component of mental wellness.

ABRAHAM MASLOW

We have only this moment, sparkling like a star in our hand . . .
and melting like a snowflake. Let us use it before it is too late.

MARIE BEYNON

Love the moment, and the energy of that moment
will spread beyond all boundaries.

CORITA KENT

Each day comes bearing its own gifts. Untie the ribbons.

RUTH ANN SCHABACKER

Normal day, let me be aware of the treasure you are.

MARY JEAN IRION

There is no such thing in anyone's life as an unimportant day. ✓

ALEXANDER WOOLLCOTT

I thank you God for this most amazing day; for the leaping
greenly spirits of trees and a blue true dream of sky; and for
everything which is natural which is infinite which is yes.

E. E. CUMMINGS

Write in your heart that every day is the best day of the year.

RALPH WALDO EMERSON

If we are ever to enjoy life, now is the time, not tomorrow or next year ... Today should always be our most wonderful day.

THOMAS DREIER

Surpassingly lively, precious days. What is there to say except: here they are. Sifting through my fingers like sand.

JOYCE CAROL OATES

Life is all memory except for the one present moment that goes by so quick you can hardly catch it going.

TENNESSEE WILLIAMS

Light tomorrow with today.

ELIZABETH BARRETT BROWNING

Whether it's the best of times or the worst of times, it's the only time we've got.

ART BUCHWALD

Forget failure

Forget past mistakes. Forget failures. Forget everything
except what you're going to do now and do it.

WILLIAM DURANT

People who soar are those who refuse to sit back, sigh and wish
things would change. They neither complain of their lot nor
passively dream of some distant ship coming in. Rather, they
visualize in their minds that they are not quitters; they will not
allow life's circumstances to push them down and hold them under.

CHARLES R. SWINDOLL

Don't wait for extraordinary opportunities.
Seize common occasions and make them great.

ORISON S. MARDEN

Far better it is to dare mighty things, to win glorious triumphs,
even though checkered by failure, than to take rank with those
poor spirits who neither enjoy much nor suffer much, because
they live in the gray twilight that knows not victory or defeat.

THEODORE ROOSEVELT

What is defeat? Nothing but education, nothing
but the first step toward something better.

WENDELL PHILLIPS

Mistakes are portals of discovery.

JAMES JOYCE

√There is nothing final about a mistake, except its being taken as final.

PHYLLIS BOTTOME

√ To lose is to learn.

ANONYMOUS

Disappointment to a noble soul is what cold water means to burning metal; it strengthens, tempers, intensifies, but never destroys it.

ELIZA TABOR

I have missed more than 9000 shots in my career. I have lost almost 300 games. On 26 occasions I have been entrusted to take the game's winning shot . . . and missed. And I have failed over and over and over again in my life. And that is why . . . I succeed.

MICHAEL JORDAN

√ You miss 100% of the shots you don't take.

WAYNE GRETZKY

Ninety-nine percent of the failures come from people who have the habit of making excuses.

GEORGE WASHINGTON CARVER

If you're gonna be a failure, at least be one at something you enjoy.

SYLVESTER STALLONE

**Failure is delay, but not defeat. It is a
temporary detour, not a dead-end street.**

WILLIAM ARTHUR WARD

**Being defeated is often a temporary condition.
Giving up is what makes it permanent.**

MARILYN VOS SAVANT

Failure is impossible.

SUSAN B. ANTHONY

Failure is the condiment that gives success its flavor.

TRUMAN CAPOTE

**Failure . . . is, in a sense, the highway to success, inasmuch
as every discovery of what is false leads us to seek earnestly
after what is true, and every fresh experience points out some
form of error which we shall afterward carefully avoid.**

JOHN KEATS

**Good people are good because they've come to wisdom through
failure. We get very little wisdom from success, you know.**

WILLIAM SAROYAN

No experiment is ever a complete failure.
It can always be used as a bad example.

PAUL DICKSON

I wasn't afraid to fail. Something good always comes out of failure.

ANNE BAXTER

What would you attempt to do if you knew you could not fail?

ROBERT SCHULLER

Gather your courage

Grow old gracefully

Courage is grace under pressure.

ERNEST HEMINGWAY

Courage is fear that has said its prayers.

RUTH FISHEL

**Courage is not the towering oak that sees storms come
and go; it is the fragile blossom that opens in the snow.**

ALICE M. SWAIM

**Courage takes many forms. There is physical courage, there is moral
courage. Then there is a still higher type of courage—the courage to brave
pain, to live with it, to never let others know of it and to still find joy in
life; to wake up in the morning with an enthusiasm for the day ahead.**

HOWARD COSELL

**You gain strength, courage and confidence by every experience in which
you really stop to look fear in the face. You are able to say to yourself,
"I lived through this horror. I can take the next thing that comes along."**

ELEANOR ROOSEVELT

**What is more mortifying than to feel that you have
missed the plum for want of courage to shake the tree?**

LOGAN PEARSALL SMITH

You can't be brave if you've only had wonderful things happen to you.

MARY TYLER MOORE

Oh God, give us serenity to accept what cannot be changed;
courage to change what should be changed, and wisdom
to distinguish the one from the other.

REINHOLD NIEBUHR

Grant me the courage not to give up even though I think it is hopeless.

CHESTER W. NIMITZ

Courage is not the absence of fear, but the mastery of it.

MARK TWAIN

The only thing we have to fear is fear itself.

FRANKLIN D. ROOSEVELT

Feel the fear, and do it anyway

SUSAN JEFFERS

Confronting your fears and allowing yourself the right to be human
can, paradoxically, make you a far happier and more productive person.

DAVID M. BURNS

Fear is a question. What are you afraid of and why? Our fears
are a treasure house of self knowledge if we explore them.

MARILYN FERGUSON

Whatever you do, you need courage. Whatever course you
decide upon, there is always someone to tell you that you are wrong.
There are always difficulties arising which tempt you to believe that
your critics are right. To map out a course of action and follow it to
the end, requires some of the same courage which a soldier needs.

RALPH WALDO EMERSON (ATTRIBUTED)

To face despair and not give in to it, that's courage.

TED KOPPEL

The greatest test of courage is to bear defeat without losing heart.

ROBERT G. INGERSOLL

There are days when you don't have a song in your heart. Sing anyway.

EMORY AUSTIN

The only courage that matters is the kind
that gets you from one moment to the next.

MIGNON McLAUGHLIN

To be courageous means to be afraid but to go a little step forward anyway.

BEVERLY SMITH

The bravest thing you can do when you are not
brave is to profess courage and act accordingly.

CORRA MAY WHITE HARRIS

Life shrinks or expands in proportion to one's courage.

ANAÏS NIN

Courage is very important. Like a muscle, it is strengthened by use.

RUTH GORDON

Courage is contagious. When a brave man takes
a stand, the spines of others are often stiffened.

BILLY GRAHAM

If you carry your childhood with you, you never become older.

ABRAHAM SUTZKEVER

Growing old is mandatory; growing up is optional.

BUMPER STICKER

✓ **You're never too old to do goofy stuff.**

WARD CLEAVER, *LEAVE IT TO BEAVER*

**Never think any oldish thoughts.
It's oldish thoughts that make a person old.**

JAMES A. FARLEY

Cancer, schmancer—as long as you're healthy.

JEWISH SAYING

**As for me, except for an occasional
heart attack, I feel as young as I ever did.**

ROBERT BENCHLEY

You can't help getting older, but you don't have to get old.

GEORGE BURNS

You're never too old to become younger.

MAE WEST

✓ **I don't know what the big deal is about old age. Old
people who shine from inside look 10 to 20 years younger.**

DOLLY PARTON

✓ **Wrinkles should merely indicate where the smiles have been.**

MARK TWAIN

Nothing is more beautiful than cheerfulness in an old face. ✓

JEAN PAUL FRIEDRICH RICHTER

I never feel age . . . If you have creative work, you don't have age or time.

LOUISE NEVELSON

**Nobody grows old by merely living a number of years.
People grow old only by deserting their ideals. Years may
wrinkle the skin, but to give up interest wrinkles the soul.**

DOUGLAS MACARTHUR

It is not the years in your life but the life in your years that counts. ✓

ADLAI STEVENSON

The best part of the art of living is to know how to grow old gracefully.

ERIC HOFFER

**Old age has a great sense of calm and freedom.
When the passions have relaxed their hold, you
have escaped not from one master but from many.**

PLATO

**The older I get, the greater power I seem to have to help the
world; I am like a snowball—the further I am rolled, the more I gain.**

SUSAN B. ANTHONY

I've always been proud of my age. I think people should be proud
they've been around long enough to have learned something.

FRANCES MOORE LAPPÉ

A new broom sweeps clean,
but an old one knows the corners.

ENGLISH SAYING

In youth we learn, in old age we understand.

MARIE VON EBNER-ESCHENBACH

One advantage in growing older is that
you can stand for more and fall for less.

MONTA CRANE

Age is opportunity no less
Than youth itself, though in another dress,
And as the evening twilight fades away
The sky is filled with stars, invisible by day.

HENRY WADSWORTH LONGFELLOW

Old age has its pleasure, which, though different,
are not less than the pleasures of youth.

W. SOMERSET MAUGHAM

There's many a good tune played on an old fiddle.

SAMUEL BUTLER

Grow along with me!
The best is yet to be,
The last of life, for which the first was made.

ROBERT BROWNING

I have no romantic feelings about age. Either you are interesting at any age or you are not. There is nothing particularly interesting about being old—or being young, for that matter.

KATHARINE HEPBURN

After thirty, a body has a mind of its own.

BETTE MIDLER

Retirement at sixty-five is ridiculous.
When I was sixty-five, I still had pimples.

GEORGE BURNS

I'm saving that rocker for the day when I feel as old as I really am.

DWIGHT D. EISENHOWER

If you rest, you rust.

HELEN HAYES

As you get older, don't slow down.
Speedup. There's less time left!

MALCOLM FORBES

The joy of being older is that in one's life, one can,
towards the end of the run, over-act appallingly.

QUENTIN CRISP

Live your life and forget your age.

FRANK BERING

To travel hopefully is a better thing than to arrive.

ROBERT LOUIS STEVENSON

Hope is the feeling you have that the feeling you have isn't permanent.

JEAN KERR

Where there's life, there's hope.

TERENCE

If it were not for hopes, the heart would break.

THOMAS FULLER

They say a person needs just three things to be truly happy in this world. Someone to love, something to do, and something to hope for.

TOM BODETT

The important thing is not that we can live on hope alone, but that life is not worth living without it.

HARVEY MILK

Man can live about forty days without food, about three days without water, about eight minutes without air . . . but only for one second without hope.

HAL LINDSEY

Hope, the best comfort of our imperfect condition.

EDWARD GIBBON

Hope, like the gleaming taper's light,
Adorns and cheers our way;
And still, as darker grows the night,
Emits a brighter ray.

OLIVER GOLDSMITH

Hope sees the invisible, feels the intangible, and achieves the impossible.

ANONYMOUS

Hope is a good thing—maybe the best thing,
and no good thing every dies.

STEPHEN KING

Look not thou down but up!

ROBERT BROWNING

The hopeful man sees success where others see failure,
sunshine where others see shadows and storm.

ORISON S. MARDEN

If winter comes, can spring be far behind?

PERCY BYSSHE SHELLEY

Flowers grow out of dark moments.

CORITA KENT

Hope is the thing with feathers that perches in the soul
and sings the tune without words and never stops at all.

EMILY DICKINSON

The gift we can offer others is so simple a thing as hope.

DANIEL BERRIGAN

There are no hopeless situations; there are only
people who have grown hopeless about them.

CLARE BOOTHE LUCE

There is no medicine like hope, no incentive so great, and
no tonic so powerful as expectation of something tomorrow.

ORISON S. MARDEN

There is one thing which gives radiance to everything.
It is the idea of something around the corner.

G. K. CHESTERTON

After all, tomorrow is another day.

MARGARET MITCHELL

Tomorrow is the most important thing in life. Comes into us at
midnight very clean. It's perfect when it arrives and it puts itself
in our hands. It hopes we've learned something from yesterday.

JOHN WAYNE

I have always been delighted at the prospect of a
new day, a fresh try, one more start, with perhaps a
bit of magic waiting somewhere behind the morning.

J. B. PRIESTLY

Just remember—when you think all is lost, the future remains.

BOB GODDARD

Keep hope alive!

JESSE JACKSON

We live very close together. So, our prime purpose in this life is
to help others. And if you can't help them, at least don't hurt them.

DALAI LAMA

No one is useless in this world who
lightens the burden of it for anyone else.

CHARLES DICKENS

God has given us two hands, one to receive
with and the other to give with.

BILLY GRAHAM

Remember, if you ever need a helping hand, you'll find one at the
end of your arm . . . As you grow older you will discover that you
have two hands. One for helping yourself, the other for helping others.

AUDREY HEPBURN

Giving is the highest expression of power.

VIVIAN GREENE

You have not done enough, you have never done enough, so
long as it is still possible that you have something to contribute.

DAG HAMMARSKJOLD

We ourselves feel that what we are doing is just a drop in the
ocean. But the ocean would be less because of that missing drop.

MOTHER TERESA

There is no exercise better for the heart
than reaching down and lifting people up.

JOHN ANDREW HOLMES, JR.

When a man is singing and cannot lift his voice, and another comes and sings with him, another who can lift his voice, the first will be able to lift his voice too. That is the secret of the bond between spirits.

HASIDIC SAYING

Whether or not we realize it each of us has within us the ability to set some kind of example for people. Knowing this would you rather be the one known for being the one who encouraged others, or the one who inadvertently discouraged those around you?

JOSH HINDS

A life isn't significant except for its impact on other lives.

JACKIE ROBINSON

Somewhere out there is a unique place for you to help others— a unique life role for you to fill that only you can fill.

THOMAS KINKADE

The sole meaning of life is to serve humanity.

LEO TOLSTOY

Long-range studies imply that doing something with other people, especially something for them, is the most powerful of all stimuli to longevity and health.

JON POPPY

From what we get, we can make a living;
what we give, however, makes a life.

ARTHUR ASHE

Service is the rent that you pay for room on this earth.

SHIRLEY CHISHOLM

Whoever renders service to many puts himself in line for greatness—great
wealth, great return, great satisfaction, great reputation, and great joy.

JIM ROHN

One thing I know: the only ones among you who will be really
happy are those who will have sought and found how to serve.

ALBERT SCHWEITZER

There is no happiness in having or in getting, but only in giving.

HENRY DRUMMOND

You give but little when you give of your possessions.
It is when you give of yourself that you truly give.

KAHLIL GIBRAN

The miracle is this—the more we share, the more we have.

LEONARD NIMOY

...the ones that give, get back in kind.

PAM DURBAN

In helping others, we shall help ourselves, for whatever
good we give out completes the circle and comes back to us.

FLORA EDWARDS

The world is good-natured to people who are good natured. ✓

WILLIAM MAKEPEACE THACKERAY

It is one of the most beautiful compensations of this life that you
cannot sincerely try to help another without helping yourself.

RALPH WALDO EMERSON

By helping yourself, you are helping mankind. By helping mankind,
you are helping yourself. That's the law of all spiritual progress.

CHRISTOPHER ISHERWOOD

If you always give, you will always have.

CHINESE PROVERB

When people are serving, life is no longer meaningless.

JOHN GARDNER

Do things for others and you'll find your self-consciousness
evaporating like morning dew on a Missouri cornfield in July.

DALE CARNEGIE

Giving opens the way to receiving.

FLORENCE SCOVEL SHINN

To serve is beautiful, but only if it is done
with joy and a whole heart and a free mind.

PEARL S. BUCK

√ You have not lived a perfect day, even though you have
earned your money, unless you have done something
for someone who will never be able to repay you.

RUTH SMELTZER

√ Real charity doesn't care if it's tax-deductible or not.

DAN BENNETT

Keep it Light

Know thyself

Angels can fly because they take themselves lightly.

G. K. CHESTERTON

Let your life lightly dance on the edges
of time like dew on the tip of a leaf.

RABINDRANATH TAGORE

The one important thing I've learned over the years is the
difference between taking one's work seriously and one's self
seriously. The first is imperative; the second is disastrous.

DAME MARGOT FONTEYN

√ Do not take life too seriously. You will never get out of it alive.

ELBERT HUBBARD

√ Sit loosely in the saddle of life.

ROBERT LOUIS STEVENSON

The bird of paradise alights only upon the hand that does not grasp.

JOHN BERRY

The willow which bends to the tempest, often escapes better than
the oak which resists it; and so in great calamities, it sometimes
happens that light and frivolous spirits recover their elasticity
and presence of mind sooner than those of a loftier character.

WALTER SCOTT

Let us be of good cheer, remembering that the misfortunes ✓
hardest to bear are those which never happen.

JAMES RUSSELL LOWELL

The game is supposed to be fun. If you have a bad day,
don't worry about it. You can't expect to get a hit every game.

YOGI BERRA

We live in an ironic society where even play is turned into work. But
the highest existence is not work; the highest level of existence is play.

CONRAD HYERS

Can you imagine experiencing the world as a great sandbox
given for us to play in like we did as children? As we play,
we can also open ourselves to the exploration of our edges,
always creating new adventures of self-exploration as we let go
of old out-dated beliefs about ourselves.

JUDITH-ANNETTE MILBURN

Life begins as a quest of the child for the man and ✓
ends as a journey by the man to rediscover the child.

LAURENS VAN DER POST

If my heart can become pure and simple like that of a child,
I think there probably can be no greater happiness than this.

KITARO NISHIDA

Great is the man who has not lost his childlike heart.

MENCIUS

To bring up a child in the way he should go,
travel that way yourself once in a while.

JOSH BILLINGS

All animals except man know that
the principal business of life is to enjoy it.

SAMUEL BUTLER

Blessed is he who has learned to laugh at himself,
for he shall never cease to be entertained.

JOHN POWELL

You should treat all disasters as if they were trivialities
but never treat a triviality as if it were a disaster.

QUENTIN CRISP

There are some things so serious you have to laugh at them.

NIELS BOHR

Jokes are better than war. Even the most aggressive jokes
are better than the least aggressive wars. Even the
longest jokes are better than the shortest wars.

GEORGE MIKES

I live by this credo: Have a little laugh and look around you for happiness instead of sadness. Laughter has always brought me out of unhappy situations. Even in your darkest moment, you usually can find something to laugh about if you try hard enough.

RED SKELTON

Happiness is not a state to arrive at, but a manner of traveling.

MARGARET LEE RUNBECK

To be happy, drop the words if only
and substitute instead the words next time.

SMILEY BLANTON

Man is unhappy because he doesn't know he's happy.
If anyone finds out he'll become happy at once.

FYODOR DOSTOYEVSKY

Make up your mind to be happy. Learn to find pleasure in simple things.

ROBERT LOUIS STEVENSON

As long as I have food and remote control, I'm happy.

MARGIE KLEIN (author's mother)

Sometimes in your life you will go on a journey. It will be the longest
journey you have ever taken. It is the journey to find yourself.

KATHERINE SHARP

Though we travel the world over to find the
beautiful, we must carry it with us or we find it not.

RALPH WALDO EMERSON

The questions which one asks oneself begin, at last, to illuminate
the world, and become one's key to the experience of others.

JAMES BALDWIN

When one is out of touch with oneself, one cannot touch others.

ANNE MORROW LINDBERGH

There is only one corner of the universe you can be
certain of improving, and that's your own self.

ALDOUS HUXLEY

Nothing can bring you peace but yourself.

RALPH WALDO EMERSON

If a man wants to be of the greatest possible value to his fellow-
creatures, let him begin the long, solitary task of perfecting himself.

ROBERTSON DAVIES

Every day, in every way, I'm getting better and better.

EMILE COUÉ

Your only obligation in any lifetime is to be true to yourself.

RICHARD BACH

What you think of yourself is much more important
than what others think of you.

SENECA

No one can make you feel inferior without your consent.

ELEANOR ROOSEVELT

Don't undermine your worth by comparing yourself with
others. It is because we are different that each of us is special.

BRIAN DYSON

Don't compromise yourself. You are all you've got.

JANIS JOPLIN

We have a mental block inside us that stops us from
earning more than we think we are worth. If we want to
earn more in reality, we have to upgrade our self-concept.

BRIAN TRACY

What you discover on your own is always more exciting than
what someone else discovers for you—it's like the difference
between romantic love and an arranged marriage.

TERENCE RAFFERTY

Know how to live within yourself: there is in your soul a whole world
of mysterious and enchanted thoughts; they will be drowned by
the noise without; daylight will drive them away;
listen to their singing and be silent.

FYODOR TYUTCHEV

All the wonders you seek are within yourself.

SIR THOMAS BROWN

I celebrate myself, and sing myself.

WALT WHITMAN

Know yourself. Don't accept your dog's admiration
as conclusive evidence that you are wonderful.

ANN LANDERS

Your vision will become clear only when you can look into your
own heart. Who looks outside, dreams; who looks inside, awakes.

CARL JUNG

Until you make peace with who you are,
you'll never be content with what you have.

DORIS MORTMAN

How many cares one loses when one decides
not to be something but to be someone.

COCO CHANEL

The important thing is this: to be able at any moment
to sacrifice what we are for what we could become.

CHARLES DU BOS

We are each gifted in a unique and important way. It is our
privilege and our adventure to discover our own special light.

MARY DUNBAR

We are the choices we make.

MERYL STREEP

Use what talents you possess; the woods would be very
silent if no birds sang except those that sang best.

HENRY VAN DYKE

Everyone has talent. What is rare is the courage
to follow the talent to the dark place where it leads.

ERICA JONG

Follow your instincts. That is where true wisdom manifests itself.

OPRAH WINFREY

Self-pity gets you nowhere. One must have the adventurous daring to accept oneself as a bundle of possibilities and undertake the most interesting game in the world—making the most of one's best.

HARRY EMERSON FOSDICK

The ultimate goal should be doing your best and enjoying it.

PEGGY FLEMING

I've always tried to do my best on the ball field. I can't do any more than that. I always try to give one hundred percent; and if my team loses, I come back and give one hundred percent the next day.

JESSE BARFIELD

Think of yourself as an athlete. I guarantee you it will change the way you stand, the way you walk, and the decisions you make about your body.

MARIAH BURTON NELSON

Do what you can, with what you have, where you are.

THEODORE ROOSEVELT

You were born an original. Don't die a copy.

JOHN MASON

To err is human, to forgive, divine.

ALEXANDER POPE

Without forgiveness life is governed by ...
an endless cycle of resentment and retaliation.

ROBERTO ASSAGIOLI

Resentment is one burden that is incompatible with your success.
Always be the first to forgive; and forgive yourself first always.

DAN ZADRA

He that cannot forgive others breaks the bridge over which
he must pass himself; for every man has need to be forgiven.

THOMAS FULLER

If you haven't forgiven yourself something, how can you forgive others?

DOLORES HUERTA

Forgive, and ye shall be forgiven.

LUKE 6:37

When a deep injury is done us, we never recover until we forgive.

ALAN PATON

To carry a grudge is like being stung to death by one bee.

WILLIAM H. WALTON

We ... need to be able to forgive, because if we don't,
we put our foot right down on the hose of our life force.

SUE PATTON THOELE

To be wronged is nothing unless you continue to remember it.

CONFUCIUS

When a man points a finger at someone else, he should
remember that three of his fingers are pointing at himself.

ANONYMOUS

Keeping score of old scores and scars, getting even
and one-upping, always makes you less than you are.

MALCOLM FORBES

Any man can seek revenge; it takes a king or prince to grant a pardon.

ARTHUR J. REHRAT

Anger makes you smaller, while forgiveness
forces you to grow beyond what you were.

CHÉRIE CARTER-SCOTT

Always forgive your enemies—nothing annoys them so much.

OSCAR WILDE

Forgiveness is a funny thing. It warms the heart and cools the sting.

WILLIAM ARTHUR WARD

Forgiveness means letting go of the past.

GERALD JAMPOLSKY

One forgives to the degree that one loves.

LA ROCHEFOUCAULD

Forgiveness is the final form of love.

REINHOLD NIEBUHR

Life is an adventure in forgiveness.

NORMAN COUSINS

I don't want to get to the end of my life and find that I lived just the length of it. I want to have lived the width of it as well.

DIANE ACKERMAN

Life is a great big canvas, and you should
throw all the paint on it you can.

DANNY KAYE

Life is a paradise for those who love many things with a passion.

LEO BUSCAGLIA

Live all you can; it's a mistake not to. It doesn't so much
matter what you do in particular, so long as you have
your life. If you haven't had that, what have you had?

HENRY JAMES

The chief danger in life is that you may take too many precautions.

ALFRED ADLER

Why not upset the apple cart? If you don't, the apples will rot anyway.

FRANK A. CLARK

I decided long ago never to look at the right hand of the menu
or the price tag of clothes—otherwise I would starve, naked.

HELEN HAYES

Everybody knows if you are too careful you are so occupied
in being careful that you are sure to stumble over something.

GERTRUDE STEIN

**If you wait for the perfect moment when all is safe
and assured, it may never arrive. Mountains will not
be climbed, races won, or lasting happiness achieved.**

MAURICE CHEVALIER

A ship in harbor is safe—but that is not what ships are for.

JOHN A. SHEDD

**Living at risk is jumping off the cliff
and building your wings on the way down.**

RAY BRADBURY

Seize the day, put no trust in tomorrow.

HORACE

Live as you will have wished to have lived when you are dying.

CHRISTIAN F. GELLERT

**At the end, you're posing for eternity. It's your
last picture. Don't be carried into death. Leap into it.**

ANATOLE BROYARD

May you live all the days of your life.

JONATHAN SWIFT

Life is ours to be spent, not to be saved.

D. H. LAWRENCE

Oh, the wild joys of living!

ROBERT BROWNING

**If you ask me what I came into this world to do,
I will tell you: I came to live out loud.**

EMILE ZOLA

Behold the tortoise. He makes progress only when he sticks his neck out.

JAMES B. CONANT

Shoot for the moon. Even if you miss it you will land among the stars.

LES BROWN

**Mama exhorted her children at every opportunity
to "jump at the sun." We might not land on
the sun, but at least we would get off the ground.**

ZORA NEALE HURSTON

**Work like you don't need money,
Love like you've never been hurt,
Sing as if no one can hear you,
And dance like no one's watching.**

ANONYMOUS

Nobody cares if you can't dance well. Just get up and dance.

DAVE BARRY

Have a blast while you last.

HOLLIS STACY

When you're skating on thin ice, you may as well tap-dance.

BRYCE COURTENAY

Don't be afraid your life will end; be afraid that it will never begin.

GRACE HANSEN

The tragedy of man is what dies inside himself while he still lives.

ALBERT SCHWEITZER

First I was dying to finish high school and start college.
And then I was dying to finish college and start working.
And then I was dying to marry and have children. And then
I was dying for my children to grow old enough so I could
return to work. And then I was dying to retire. And now,
I am dying ... And suddenly realize I forgot to live.

ANONYMOUS

One of the most tragic things I know about human nature
is that all of us tend to put off living. We are all dreaming
of some magical rose garden over the horizon—instead of
enjoying the roses blooming outside our windows today.

DALE CARNEGIE

Don't hurry, don't worry. You're only here for a
short visit. So be sure to stop and smell the flowers.

WALTER HAGEN

It's only when we truly know and understand that we
have a limited time on earth—and that we have no way
of knowing when our time is up—that we will begin to
live each day to the fullest, as if it was the only one we had.

ELISABETH KÜBLER-ROSS

Live each day as you would climb a mountain . . . Climb slowly,
steadily, enjoying each passing moment; and the view from
the summit will serve as a fitting climax for the journey.

HAROLD V. MELCHERT

When a child is born, all rejoice; when someone dies, all weep. But it makes just as much sense, if not more, to rejoice at the end of a life as at the beginning. For no one can tell what events await a newborn child, but when a mortal dies he has successfully completed a journey.

TALMUD

We don't receive wisdom; we must discover it for ourselves after a journey that no one can take for us or spare us.

MARCEL PROUST

Either control your own destiny, or someone else will!

JOHN F. WELCH, JR.

Destiny is not a matter of chance, it is a matter of choice; it is not a thing to be waited for, it is a thing to be achieved.

WILLIAM JENNINGS BRYAN

We must be willing to get rid of the life we've planned, so as to have the life that is waiting for us.

JOSEPH CAMPBELL

If we trust our intuition and respond, it's always right, because we're open enough to see what to do.

PAUL HORN

Every person, all the events of your life are there because you have drawn them there. What you choose to do with them is up to you.

RICHARD BACH

The greatest use of life is to spend it for something that will outlast it.

WILLIAM JAMES

Here is a test to find whether your mission on earth is finished: if you're alive, it isn't.

RICHARD BACH

The game of life is not so much in holding a good hand as playing a poor hand well.

H. T. LESLIE

All the art of living lies in a fine mingling of letting go and holding on.

HAVELOCK ELLIS

Life is a movie you see through your own, unique eyes. It makes little difference what's happening out there. It's how you take it that counts.

DENIS WAITLEY

Life moves pretty fast; if you don't stop and look around every once in a while, you could miss it.

JOHN HUGHES

It is good to have an end to journey toward;
but it is the journey that matters, in the end.

Ursula K. Le Guin

Life is like a sewer—you get out of it what you put into it.

Tom Lehrer

Things turn out best for the people who
make the best of the way things turn out.

John Wooden

Life doesn't require that we do
the best—only that we try our best.

H. Jackson Brown, Jr.

Life does not have to be perfect to be wonderful.

Annette Funicello

When things go wrong, as they sometimes will,
When the road you're trudging seems all up hill,
. . . When care is pressing you down a bit,
Rest, if you must—but don't you quit.

ANONYMOUS

Be like a postage stamp—stick to one thing till you get there.

JOSH BILLINGS

If you really want something, you can figure out how to make it happen.

CHER

Don't give up when you still have something to give.
Nothing is really over until the moment you stop trying.

BRIAN DYSON

You may be disappointed if you fail, but you are doomed if you don't try.

BEVERLY SILLS

The important thing is to learn a lesson every time you lose.

JOHN MCENROE

Problems are messages.

SHAKTI GAWAIN

A setback is the opportunity to begin again more intelligently.

HENRY FORD

Giving up is the ultimate tragedy.

ROBERT J. DONOVAN

It is common sense to take a method and try it. If it fails, admit it frankly and try another. But above all, try something.

FRANKLIN D. ROOSEVELT

Never let your head hang down. Never give up and sit down and grieve. Find another way.

SATCHEL PAIGE

Fall seven times, stand up eight.

JAPANESE PROVERB

Our greatest glory is not in never falling, but in rising every time we fall.

CONFUCIUS

A bend in the road is not the end of the road . . . unless you fail to make the turn.

ANONYMOUS

If you have made mistakes there is always another chance. You may have a fresh start any moment you choose, for this thing we call "failure" is not the falling down, but the staying down.

MARY PICKFORD

I think a hero is an ordinary individual who finds the strength to persevere and endure in spite of overwhelming obstacles.

CHRISTOPHER REEVE

Keep on keepin' on.

POPULAR SAYING

Little by little does the trick.

AESOP

By perseverance the snail reached the ark.

CHARLES HADDON SPURGEON

In the confrontation between the stream and the rock, the stream always wins ... not through strength, but through persistence.

ANONYMOUS

The flower that follows the sun does so even on cloudy days.

ROBERT LEIGHTON

Even the woodpecker owes his success to the fact that he uses
his head and keeps pecking away until he finishes the job he starts.

COLEMAN COX

Adopt the pace of nature: her secret is patience.

RALPH WALDO EMERSON

The key to everything is patience. You get the
chicken by hatching the egg—not by smashing it.

ARNOLD GLASOW

With time and patience the mulberry leaf becomes a silk gown.

CHINESE PROVERB

I think and think for months and years. Ninety-nine times,
the conclusion is false. The hundredth time I am right.

ALBERT EINSTEIN

Champions keep playing until they get it right.

BILLY JEAN KING

It's easy to have faith in yourself and have discipline
when you're a winner, when you're number one. What you
got to have is faith and discipline when you're not a winner.

VINCE LOMBARDI

Never confuse a single defeat with a final defeat.

F. Scott Fitzgerald

It's never too late, in fiction or in life, to revise.

Nancy Thayer

Overcome obstacles

Sometimes things which at the moment may be perceived as obstacles—and actually be obstacles, difficulties, or drawbacks—can in the long run result in some good end which would not have occurred if it had no been for the obstacle.

STEVE ALLEN

The world is round and the place which may seem like the end may also be only the beginning.

GEORGE BAKER

What the caterpillar calls the end of the world, the master calls a butterfly.

RICHARD BACH

Difficulties are meant to rouse, not discourage. The human spirit is to grow strong by conflict.

WILLIAM ELLERY CHANNING

Adversity causes some men to break; others to break records.

WILLIAM ARTHUR WARD

I would never have amounted to anything were it not for adversity. I was forced to come up the hard way.

J. C. PENNEY

I have found that life persists in the midst of destruction and, therefore, there must be a higher law than that of destruction.

MAHATMA GANDHI

Life is a series of experiences, each one of which makes
us bigger, even though sometimes it is hard to realize this.

HENRY FORD

The difficulties, hardships and trials of life, the obstacles . . . are positive
blessings. They knit the muscles more firmly, and teach self-reliance.

WILLIAM MATTHEW

Should you shield the canyons from the windstorms,
you would never see the beauty of their carvings.

ELISABETH KUBLER-ROSS

The more the marble wastes, the more the statue grows.

MICHELANGELO

If all our misfortunes were laid in one common heap
whence everyone must take an equal portion, most
people would be contented to take their own and depart.

SOCRATES

The more you try to avoid suffering, the more you suffer because
smaller things begin to torture you in proportion to your fear of suffering.

THOMAS MERTON

To live is too suffer, to survive is to find meaning in suffering.

VIKTOR FRANKL

Even in the deepest sinking there is the hidden purpose of an ultimate rising. Thus it is for all men; from none is the source of light withheld unless he himself withdraws from it. Therefore the most important thing is not to despair.

HASIDIC SAYING

Don't get hung up on a snag in the stream, my dear. Snags alone are not so dangerous—it's the debris that clings to them that makes the trouble. Pull yourself loose and go on.

ANNE SHANNON MONROE

Anyone can carry his burden, however heavy, until nightfall. Anyone can do his work, however hard, for one day. Anyone can live sweetly, patiently, lovingly, purely, till the sun goes down and that is all that life really means.

ROBERT LOUIS STEVENSON

Nothing happens to anybody which he is not fitted by nature to bear.

MARCUS AURELIUS

What does not destroy me, makes me strong.

FRIEDRICH NIETZSCHE

No tree becomes rooted and sturdy unless many a wind assails it. For by its very tossing in tightens its grip and plants its roots more securely; the fragile trees are those that have grown in a sunny valley.

SENECA

Nothing splendid has ever been achieved except
by those who dared believe that something inside them
was superior to circumstance.

BRUCE BARTON

I seldom think about my limitations, and they never
make me sad. Perhaps there is just a touch of yearning
at times; but it is vague, like a breeze among flowers.

HELEN KELLER

They never told me I couldn't.

TOM DEMPSEY

Some misfortunes we bring upon ourselves; others are
completely beyond our control. But no matter what happens
to us, we always have some control over what we do about it.

SUZY SZASZ

The longer we dwell on our misfortunes,
the greater is their power to harm us.

VOLTAIRE

Trouble is a part of life, and if you don't share it, you don't give
the person who loves you enough chance to love you enough.

DINAH SHORE

It's easy enough to be pleasant when everything goes
like a song, but the man who is worthwhile is the
man who can smile when everything goes dead wrong.

ANONYMOUS

Weeping may endure for a night, but joy cometh in the morning.

PSALMS 30:5

The only way to get through whatever olympics we're
engaged in is by firing up a sense of humor and pressing on.

JAMES KIRKWOOD

We become so overwhelmed by illness, death and grief that we
forget that humor, like the moon, can bring light to our darkest times.

ALLEN KLEIN

By their merry talk they cause sufferers to forget grief.

TALMUD

Turn your stumbling blocks into stepping stones.

ANONYMOUS

Knock the *t* off the *can't*.

GEORGE REEVES

**We are continually faced by great opportunities
brilliantly disguised as insoluble problems.**

LEE IOCOCCA

**There are no great people in this world, only great
challenges which ordinary people rise to meet.**

WILLIAM FREDERICK HALSEY, JR.

Trouble is only opportunity in work clothes.

HENRY J. KAISER

**I will love the light for it shows me the way. Yet I
will endure the darkness for it shows me the stars.**

OG MANDINO

**Do not think of today's failures, but of the success that may come
tomorrow. You have set yourselves a difficult task, but you will succeed
if you persevere; and you will find a joy in overcoming obstacles.**

HELEN KELLER

**Achieving goals by themselves will never make us happy
in the long term: it's who you become, as you overcome the
obstacles necessary to achieve your goals, that can give you
the deepest sense and most long-lasting sense of fulfillment.**

TONY ROBBINS

Difficult times have helped me to understand better than before how
infinitely rich and beautiful life is in every way and that so many
things that one goes worrying about are of no importance whatsoever.

ISAK DINESEN

If you break your neck, if you have nothing to eat,
if your house is on fire—then you got a problem.
Everything else is inconvenience.

ROBERT FULGHUM

Right Livelihood

Your work is to discover your work and
then with all your heart to give yourself to it.

THE BUDDHA

The first step is to find out what you love—and don't be
practical about it. The second step is to start doing
what you love immediately, in any small way possible.

BARBARA SHER

All work is empty save when there is love.

KAHLIL GIBRAN

To love what you do and feel that it matters—
how could anything else be more fun?

KATHARINE GRAHAM

Where our work is, there let our joy be.

TERTULLIAN

A musician must make music, an artist must paint,
a poet must write, if he is to be ultimately at peace
with himself. What a man can be, he must be.

ABRAHAM MASLOW

Blessed is he who has found his work.

THOMAS CARLYLE

Every individual has a place to fill in the world and is
important in some respect whether he chooses to be so or not.

NATHANIEL HAWTHORNE

Work is love made visible. And if you cannot work with love but
only with distaste, it is better that you should leave your work and sit
at the gate of the temple and take alms of those who work with joy.

KAHLIL GIBRAN

God gave man work, not to burden him, but to bless him,
and useful work, willingly, cheerfully, effectively done,
has always been the finest expression of the human spirit.

WALTER R. COURTENAY

None of us will ever accomplish anything excellent or commanding
except when he listens to this whisper which is heard by him alone.

RALPH WALDO EMERSON

The greatness of work is inside man.

POPE JOHN PAUL II

All labor that uplifts humanity has dignity and importance
and should be undertaken with painstaking excellence.

MARTIN LUTHER KING, JR.

There is as much dignity in tilling a field as in writing a poem.

BOOKER T. WASHINGTON

There are no menial jobs, only menial attitudes.

WILLIAM J. BENNETT

Honest labor bears a lovely face.

THOMAS DEKKER

I do not like work—no man does—but I like what is in
work—the chance to find yourself. Your own reality—for
yourself, not for others—what no other man can ever know.

JOSEPH CONRAD

Life means to have something definite to do—a mission
to fulfill—and in the measure in which we avoid setting
our life to something, we make it empty. Human life,
by its very nature, has to be dedicated to something.

JOSÉ ORTEGA Y GASSET

Far and away the best prize that life offers is
the chance to work hard at work worth doing.

THEODORE ROOSEVELT

**If a man hasn't discovered something
that he would die for, he isn't fit to live.**

MARTIN LUTHER KING, JR.

**Sometimes it is more important to discover
what one cannot do, than what one can do.**

LIN YUTANG

**Work is effort applied toward some end. The most satisfying work
involves directing our efforts toward achieving ends that we
ourselves endorse as worthy expressions of our talent and character.**

WILLIAM J. BENNETT

**Let us not be content to wait and see what will happen, but
give us the determination to make the right things happen.**

PETER MARSHALL

**The return from your work must be the satisfaction which that work
brings you and the world's need of that work. With that, life is heaven, or
as near heaven as you can get. Without this—with work which you despise,
which bores you, and which the world does not need—this life is hell.**

W. E. B. DU BOIS

We become what we do.

CHIANG KAI-SHEK

It's no good running a pig farm badly for thirty years while saying,
"Really I was meant to be a ballet dancer." By that time,
pigs will be your style.

QUENTIN CRISP

Let each man pass his days in that wherein his skill is greatest.

SEXTUS PROPERTIUS

Destiny is what you are supposed to do in life.
Fate is what kicks you in the ass to make you do it.

HENRY MILLER

Work has to include our deepest values and passions and
feelings and commitments, or it's not work, it's just a job.

MATTHEW FOX

Anybody can do just about anything with himself
that he really wants to and makes up his mind to do.
We are capable of greater things than we realize.

NORMAN VINCENT PEALE

Do What You Love, The Money Will Follow

MARSHA SINETAR

Sweet smell of success

Don't aim for success if you want it; just do what
you love and believe in, and it will come naturally.

DAVID FROST

Success follows doing what you want to do.
There is no other way to be successful.

MALCOLM FORBES

Know what you want to do, hold the thought firmly,
and do every day what should be done, and
every sunset will see you that much nearer the goal.

ELBERT HUBBARD

Every successful person I have heard of has done the best he could with
the conditions as he found them, and not waited until next year for better.

E. W. HOWE

It takes twenty years to make an overnight success.

EDDIE CANTOR

Perseverance is a great element of success. If you only knock long
enough and loud enough at the gate, you are sure to wake up somebody.

HENRY WADSWORTH LONGFELLOW

The elevator to success is out of order. You'll
have to use the stairs ... one step at a time.

JOE GIRARD

Success seems to be largely a matter
of hanging on after others have let go.

WILLIAM FEATHER

Most people who succeed in the face of seemingly impossible
conditions are people who simply don't know how to quit.

ROBERT SCHULLER

Character cannot be developed in ease and quiet. Only
through experience of trial and suffering can the soul be
strengthened, ambition inspired, and success achieved.

HELEN KELLER

I cannot give you the formula for success, but I can give you
the formula for failure, which is: Try to please everybody.

HERBERT B. SWOPE

You always pass failure on the way to success.

MICKEY ROONEY

If you're not failing now and again, it's a sign you're playing it safe.

WOODY ALLEN

The difference between good and great is just a little extra effort.

DUFFY DAUGHERTY

If you aren't going all the way, why go at all?

JOE NAMATH

Success is not the result of spontaneous combustion.
You must first set yourself on fire.

FRED SHERO

People become really quite remarkable when they start
thinking that they can do things. When they believe
in themselves they have the first secret of success.

NORMAN VINCENT PEALE

While one person hesitates because he feels inferior, the
other is busy making mistakes and becoming superior.

HENRY C. LINK

I studied the lives of great men and famous women, and
I found that the men and women who get to the top were
those who did the jobs they had in hand, with everything
they had of energy and enthusiasm and hard work.

HARRY S TRUMAN

Keep away from people who try to belittle your
ambitions. Small people always do that, but the really
great make you feel that you, too, can become great.

MARK TWAIN

Whenever you're sitting across from some important
person, always picture him sitting there in a suit of long
underwear. That's the way I always operated in business.

JOSEPH P. KENNEDY

Everything depends upon circumstances:
you must sail according to the wind.

PICONNERIE DE LA BUGEAUD

Don't wait for your ship to come; swim out to it.

ANONYMOUS

Find a need and fill it.

HENRY J. KAISER

The secret to success in life is for a man to be
ready for his opportunity when it comes.

BENJAMIN DISRAELI

If a window of opportunity appears don't pull down the shade.

TOM PETERS

If opportunity doesn't knock, build a door.

MILTON BERLE

**Don't be afraid to take a big step if one is indicated.
You can't cross a chasm in two small jumps.**

DAVID LLOYD GEORGE

**There are some things one can only achieve
by a deliberate leap in the opposite direction.**

FRANZ KAFKA

**Why should we be in such desperate haste to succeed, and in such
desperate enterprises? If a man does not keep pace with his
companions, perhaps it is because he hears a different drummer.**

HENRY DAVID THOREAU

Success consists of getting up just one more time than you fall.

OLIVER GOLDSMITH

Genius is one percent inspiration and ninety-nine percent perspiration.

THOMAS A. EDISON

Eighty percent of success is showing up.

WOODY ALLEN

The secret of success is constancy to purpose.

BENJAMIN DISRAELI

**The world stands aside to let anyone
pass who knows where he is going.**

DAVID STARR JORDAN

**Winners can tell you where they are going, what they plan to do
along the way, and who will be sharing the adventure with them.**

DENIS WAITLEY

**Success means we go to sleep at night knowing that our
talents and abilities were used in a way that served others.**

MARIANNE WILLIAMSON

**If a man has a talent and cannot use it, he has failed. If he has a
talent and uses only half of it, he has partially failed. If he has a talent
and learns somehow to use the whole of it, he has gloriously
succeeded, and won a satisfaction and a triumph few men ever know.**

THOMAS WOLFE

The richest person is the one who is contented with what he has. ✓

ROBERT C. SAVAGE

Abundance is about being rich, with or without money.

SUZE ORMAN

Money may be the husk of many things, but not the kernel. It brings you food, but not appetite; medicine, but not health; acquaintances, but not friends; servants, but not loyalty; days of joy, but not peace or happiness.

HENRIK IBSEN

He has achieved success who has lived well,
laughed often and loved much.

ELBERT HUBBARD

No man is a failure who is enjoying life.

WILLIAM FEATHER

I'd rather be a failure at something I enjoy
than be a success at something I hate.

GEORGE BURNS

Most people can do extraordinary things if they have the confidence or take the risks. Yet most people don't. They sit in front of the telly and treat life as if it goes on forever.

PHILIP ADAMS

God gave us two ends. One to sit on and one to think with. Success depends on which one you use; heads, you win—tails, you lose.

ANONYMOUS

Take the first step

A journey of a thousand miles must begin with a single step.

CHINESE PROVERB

What saves a man is to take a step. Then another step.

ANTOINE DE SAINT-EXUPÉRY

The distance is nothing. It's only the first step that's important.

MARQUISE DU DEFFAND

He who has begun has half done. Dare to be wise; begin!

HORACE

Begin somewhere; you cannot build a
reputation on what you intend to do.

LIZ SMITH

No matter how big or soft or warm
your bed is, you still have to get out of it.

GRACE SLICK

The beginning is the most important part of the work.

PLATO

Don't wait for something big to occur. Start
where you are, with what you have, and that
will always lead you into something greater.

MARY MANIN MORRISSEY

The person who moves a mountain
begins by carrying away small stones.

CHINESE PROVERB

The older I get, the more wisdom I find in the ancient rule of
taking first things first—a process which often reduces the
most complex human problems to manageable proportions.

DWIGHT D. EISENHOWER

The secret of getting ahead is getting started. The secret of
getting started is breaking your complex overwhelming tasks
into small manageable tasks, and then starting on the first one.

MARK TWAIN

You can't try to do things; you simply must do them.

RAY BRADBURY

The tragedy of life is not that it ends so
soon, but that we wait so long to begin it.

ANONYMOUS

Inaction may be the biggest form of action.

JERRY BROWN

**If you don't know where you are going,
you will probably end up somewhere else.**

LAURENCE J. PETER

The important thing is somehow to begin.

HENRY MOORE

As long as you can start, you are all right. The juice will come.

ERNEST HEMINGWAY

**Often people attempt to live their lives backwards; they try
to have more things, or more money, in order to do more of
what they want, so they will be happier. The way it actually
works is the reverse. You must first be who you really are,
then do what you need to do, in order to have what you want.**

MARGARET YOUNG

Knowing what you want is the first step to getting it.

LOUISE HART

**Where we stand is not as important
as the direction in which we are going.**

OLIVER WENDELL HOLMES, JR.

If you're climbing the ladder of life, you go rung by rung, one step
at a time ... Sometimes you don't think you're progressing
until you step back and see how high you've really gone.

DONNY OSMOND

Never look down to test the ground before taking your next step; only
he who keeps his eye fixed on the far horizon will find his right road.

DAG HAMMARSKJOLD

"Begin at the beginning," the king said, gravely,
"and go till you come to the end; then stop."

LEWIS CARROLL

Win some, lose some

You're gonna lose some ballgames and you're gonna win some ballgames and that's about it.

SPARKY ANDERSON

For everything you have missed, you have gained something else; and for everything you gain, you lose something.

RALPH WALDO EMERSON

Sometimes things can go right only by first going very wrong.

EDWARD TENNER

There are many in this old world of ours who hold that things break about even for all of us. I have observed for example that we all get the same amount of ice. The rich get it in the summertime and the poor get it in the winter.

BAT MASTERSON

Life is pretty simple: You do some stuff. Most fails. Some works. You do more of what works. If it works big, others quickly copy it. Then you do something else. The trick is the doing something else.

TOM PETERS

Victory is not won in miles but in inches. Win a little now, hold your ground, and later win a little more.

LOUIS L'AMOUR

If you think you can win, you can win. Faith is necessary to victory.

WILLIAM HAZLITT

Pick battles big enough to matter, small enough to win.

JONATHAN KOZOL

If it was a worthwhile fight, it didn't matter
who won; some good was sure to come of it.

RICHARD BROOKS

When you let someone else win an
argument, often you both end up winners.

RICHARD CARLSON

The person who upsets you the most is your best teacher,
because they bring you face to face with who you are.

LYNN ANDREWS

Some people like me. Some people don't. You can never
get everyone to like you, so why knock yourself out trying?

CLAUDETTE COLBERT

Winners never quit and quitters never win.

VINCE LOMBARDI

You really never lose until you stop trying.

MIKE DITKA

Everything that has a beginning has an ending.
Make your peace with that and all will be well.

THE BUDDHA

The Lift-Your-Spirits Quote Book

A powerful agent
is the right word.

MARK TWAIN

Applause

Arts

Art • Dance • Music • Poetry

When someone does something well, applaud!
You will make two people happy.

SAMUEL GOLDWYN

He who praises another enriches himself far more than
he does the one praised. To praise is an investment in
happiness. The poorest human being has something to
give that the richest could not buy.

GEORGE MATTHEW ADAMS

The way to develop the best that is in a man
is by appreciation and encouragement.

CHARLES SCHWAB

The applause of a single human being is of great consequence.

SAMUEL JOHNSON

Most people like praise . . . When it is really deserved,
most people expand under it into richer and better selves.

JOSEPH FARRELL

The sweetest of all sounds is praise.

XENOPHON

Down deep we really know our worth, but we don't have easy access
to that knowledge. We need to hear praise coming from outside
ourselves or we won't remember that we deserve it.

BARBARA SHER

Find the good—and praise it.

ALEX HALEY

Every day, tell at least one person something
you like, admire, or appreciate about them.

RICHARD CARLSON

Judicious praise is to children what the sun is to flowers.

CHRISTIAN BOVEE

A little praise
Goes a great ways.

RALPH WALDO EMERSON

**Art is much less important than life,
but what a poor life without it.**

ROBERT MOTHERWELL

Art washes away from the soul the dust of everyday life.

PABLO PICASSO

**Without art, the crudeness of reality
would make the world unbearable.**

GEORGE BERNARD SHAW

**Art is a staple, like bread or wine or a warm coat in winter.
Man's spirit grows hungry for art in the same way
his stomach growls for food.**

IRVING STONE

The object of art is to give life a shape.

JEAN ANOUILH

**The artist has a special task and duty; the task of reminding
men of their humanity and the promise of their creativity.**

LEWIS MUMFORD

Each of us is an artist, capable of conceiving
and creating a vision from the depths of our being.

DOROTHY FADIMAN

All that is good in art is the expression of one soul talking to another;
and is precious according to the greatness of the soul that utters it.

JOHN RUSKIN

The artist alone sees spirits. But after he has told
of their appearing to him, everybody sees them.

GOETHE

Artists are nearest God. Into their souls he breathes his life, and from
their hands it comes in fair, articulate forms to bless the world.

JOSIAH GILBERT HOLLAND

A work of art has an author and yet, when it is perfect,
it has something which is anonymous about it.

SIMONE WEIL

The true work of art is but a shadow of the divine perfection.

MICHELANGELO

The artist is the confidant of nature, flowers carry on dialogues with him through the graceful bending of their stems and the harmoniously tinted nuances of their blossoms. Every flower has a cordial word which nature directs towards him.

AUGUSTE RODIN

There are painters who transform the sun to a yellow spot, but there are others who with the help of their art and their intelligence, transform a yellow spot into sun.

PABLO PICASSO

Science and art have that in common that everyday things seem to them new and attractive.

FRIEDRICH NIETZSCHE

Art arises when the secret vision of the artist and the manifestation of nature agree to find new shapes.

KAHLIL GIBRAN

Learning to draw is really a matter of learning to see—to see correctly—and that means a good deal more than merely looking with the eye.

KIMON NICOLAIDES

Drawing is the discipline by which I constantly rediscover the world. I have learned that what I have not drawn, I have never really seen, and that when I start drawing an ordinary thing, I realize how extraordinary it is, sheer miracle.

FREDERICK FRANCK

I shut my eyes in order to see.

PAUL GAUGUIN

Dancing is the loftiest, the most moving, the most beautiful of the arts, because it is no mere translation or abstraction from life; it is life itself.

HAVELOCK ELLIS

The body says what words cannot.

MARTHA GRAHAM

Dancing is the body made poetic.

ERNST BACON

**The trouble with nude dancing is that
not everything stops when the music stops.**

SIR ROBERT HELPMANN

Let that day be lost to us on which we did not dance once!

FRIEDRICH NIETZSCHE

If you can walk, you can dance.

ZIMBABWE SAYING

Music is well said to be the speech of angels.

THOMAS CARLYLE

Music is the child of prayer, the companion of religion.

CHATEAUBRIAND

**Music is the art of the prophets, the only art that can calm
the agitations of the soul; it is one of the most magnificent
and delightful presents God has given us.**

MARTIN LUTHER

Musical training is a more potent instrument
than any other, because rhythm and harmony
find their way into the inward places of the soul.

PLATO

We are full of rhythms . . . our pulse, our gestures,
our digestive tracts, the lunar and seasonal cycles.

YEHUDI MENUHIN

When I hear music, I fear no danger. I am invulnerable.
I see no foe. I am related to the earliest times, and to the latest.

HENRY DAVID THOREAU

The best, most beautiful, and most perfect way that we have
of expressing a sweet concord of mind to each other is by music.

JONATHAN EDWARDS

When words leave off, music begins.

HEINRICH HEINE

After silence that which comes nearest
to expressing the inexpressible is music.

ALDOUS HUXLEY

Music is the universal language of mankind.

HENRY WADSWORTH LONGFELLOW

There is no feeling, except the extremes of fear
and grief that does not find relief in music.

GEORGE ELIOT

Without music, life is a journey through a desert.

PAT CONROY

I merely took the energy it takes to pout and wrote some blues.

DUKE ELLINGTON

God respects me when I work, but loves me when I sing.

RABINDRANATH TAGORE

We all have music inside us, and can learn
how to get it out, one way or another.

FRANK WILSON

Poetry ennobles the heart and the eyes, and unveils the meaning of
all things upon which the heart and the eyes dwell. It discovers the
secret rays of the universe, and restores to us forgotten paradises.

EDITH SITWELL

To read a poem in January is as lovely
as to go for a walk in June.

JEAN PAUL

Poetry is something to make us wiser and better,
by continually revealing those types of beauty and truth,
which God has set in all men's souls.

JAMES RUSSELL LOWELL

The poem is a little myth of man's capacity of making his life
meaningful. And in the end, the poem is not a thing we see—it is,
rather, a light by which we may see—and what we see is life.

ROBERT PENN WARREN

Poetry is the utterance of deep and heartfelt truth.
The true poet is very near the oracle.

EDWARD HUBBELL CHAPIN

The poets are only the interpreters of the gods.

SOCRATES

Poetry is simply the most beautiful, impressive,
and widely effective mode of saying things.

MATTHEW ARNOLD

When power narrows the area of man's concern, poetry
reminds him of the richness and diversity of his existence.

JOHN F. KENNEDY

When you read and understand a poem, comprehending its
rich and formal meanings, then you master chaos a little.

STEPHEN SPENDER

There is as much dignity in tilling
a field as in writing a poem.

BOOKER T. WASHINGTON

You will find poetry nowhere unless
you bring some of it with you.

JOSEPH JOUBERT

Beauty

Beauty is in the eye of the beholder.

MARGARET HUNGERFORD

**Some thoughts always find us young, and keep us so.
Such a thought is the love of the universal and eternal beauty.**

RALPH WALDO EMERSON

Anyone who keeps the ability to see beauty never grows old.

FRANZ KAFKA

**Let the beauty you love be what you do.
There are a thousand ways to kneel and kiss the earth.**

RUMI

Beautiful is greater than Good, for it includes the Good.

GOETHE

**The most natural beauty in the world is honesty
and moral truth. For all beauty is truth.**

LORD SHAFTESBURY

To do the useful thing, to say the courageous thing,
to contemplate the beautiful thing:
that is enough for one man's life.

T. S. ELIOT

I'm tired of all the nonsense about beauty being only skin-deep.
That's deep enough. What do you want—an adorable pancreas?

JEAN KERR

The fountain of beauty is the heart, and every
generous thought illustrates the walls of your chamber.

FRANCIS QUARLES

Beauty as we feel it is something indescribable;
what it is or what it means can never be said.

GEORGE SANTAYANA

Things are beautiful if you love them.

JEAN ANOUILH

There is certainly no absolute standard of beauty.
That precisely is what makes its pursuit so interesting.

JOHN KENNETH GALBRAITH

A thing of beauty is a joy forever.

JOHN KEATS

**When your inner eyes open, you can find immense
beauty hidden within the inconsequential details of daily
life. When your inner ears open, you can hear the subtle,
lovely music of the universe everywhere you go.**

TIMOTHY RAY MILLER

**Though we travel the world over to find the beautiful,
we must carry it with us or we will not find it.**

RALPH WALDO EMERSON

God is in the world, or nowhere, creating continually in us and around us. Insofar as man partakes of this creative process does he partake of the divine, of God, and that participation is his immortality . . . .

ALFRED NORTH WHITEHEAD

You were placed on this earth
to create, not to compete.

ROBERT ANTHONY

Every moment of your life is infinitely creative and the universe is endlessly bountiful. Just put forth a clear enough request, and everything your heart truly desires must come to you.

SHAKTI GAWAIN

There is no greater joy than that of feeling oneself a creator. The triumph of life is expressed by creation.

HENRI BERGSON

Creativity is a central source of meaning in our lives . . . most of the things that are interesting, important, and human are the results of creativity . . . when we are involved in it, we feel that we are living more fully than during the rest of life.

MIHALY CSIKSZENTMIHALYI

**Creativeness often consists of merely
turning up what is already there.**

BERNICE FITZ-GIBBON

A hunch is creativity trying to tell you something.

FRANK CAPRA

**I saw an angel in the block of marble
and I just chiseled 'til I set him free.**

MICHELANGELO

**In creating, the only hard thing's to begin;
A grass-blade's no easier to make than an oak.**

JAMES RUSSELL LOWELL

**No matter how old you get, if you can keep the desire
to be creative, you're keeping the man-child alive.**

JOHN CASSAVETES

**It is the child in man that is the source of his uniqueness
and creativeness, and the playground is the optimal milieu
for the unfolding of his capacities.**

ERIC HOFFER

Many times we will get more ideas and better ideas
in two hours of creative loafing than in eight hours at a desk.

WILFRED PETERSON

If you are seeking creative ideas, go out walking.
Angels whisper to a man when he goes for a walk.

RAYMOND INMAN

Family

Babies

Children

Parents

Grandparents

Friendship

The whole world is my family.

POPE JOHN XXIII

**To us, family means putting your arms
around each other and being there.**

BARBARA BUSH

**The happiest moments of my life have been the few
which I have passed at home in the bosom of my family.**

THOMAS JEFFERSON

The family with an old person in it possesses a jewel.

CHINESE SAYING

Babies are such a nice way to start people.

DON HEROLD

**Each time a new baby is born there is a possibility of reprieve.
Each child is a new being, a potential prophet, a new spiritual
prince, a new spark of light precipitated into the outer darkness.**

R. D. LAING

Every baby born into the world is a finer one than the last.

CHARLES DICKENS

The infant is music itself.

HAZRAT INAYAT KHAN

When the first baby laughed for the first time, the laugh broke into a thousand pieces and they all went skipping about, and that was the beginning of fairies.

J. M. BARRIE

A baby is God's opinion that life should go on.

CARL SANDBURG

**Children are God's apostles, day by day
Sent forth to preach of love, and hope, and peace.**

JAMES RUSSELL LOWELL

**Every child comes with the message
that God is not yet discouraged of man.**

RABINDRANATH TAGORE

Bringing a child into the world is the greatest act of hope there is.

LOUISE HART

**Children are the world's most valuable
resource and its best hope for the future.**

JOHN F. KENNEDY

**Blessed be childhood, which brings down something of
heaven into the midst of our rough earthliness.**

HENRI AMIEL

Children are the bridge to heaven.

PERSIAN PROVERB

We are given children to test us and make us more spiritual.

GEORGE WILL

One laugh of a child will make the holiest day more sacred still.

ROBERT G. INGERSOLL

**Children are the true connoisseurs.
What's precious to them has no price—only value.**

BEL KAUFMAN

There are no seven wonders of the world
in the eyes of a child. There are seven million.

WALT STREIGHTIFF

Children, like animals, use all their senses to discover the world.
Then artists come along and discover it the same way all over again.

EUDORA WELTY

The only artists for whom I would make way are—children.
For me the paintings of children belong side by side with
the works of the masters.

HENRY MILLER

Every child is an artist.
The problem is how to remain an artist once he grows up.

PABLO PICASSO

Every child is born a genius.

R. BUCKMINSTER FULLER

Why, a four-year-old child could understand this report.
Run out and find me a four-year-old child.

GROUCHO MARX

Adults are always asking little kids what they want to be when
they grow up—'cause they're looking for ideas.

PAULA POUNDSTONE

What do we teach our children? . . . We should say to each of them:
Do you know what you are? You are a marvel. You are unique . . .
You may become a Shakespeare, a Michelangelo, a Beethoven.
You have the capacity for anything.

PABLO CASALS

By giving children lots of affection, you can help fill them
with love and acceptance of themselves.
Then that's what they will have to give away.

WAYNE DYER

Teaching kids to count is fine,
but teaching them what counts is best.

BOB TALBERT

It is infinitely more useful for a child to hear a story told
by a person than by computer. Because the greatest part of the
learning experience lies not in the particular words of the story
but in the involvement with the individual reading it.

FRANK SMITH

The parents exist to teach the child, but also they must learn what the child has to teach them; and the child has a very great deal to teach them.

ARNOLD BENNETT

Grown men can learn from very little children for the hearts of little children are pure. Therefore, the Great Spirit may show to them many things which older people miss.

BLACK ELK

Children have a remarkable talent for not taking the adult world with the kind of respect we are so confident it ought to be given. To the irritation of authority figures of all sorts, children expend considerable energy in "clowning around." They refuse to appreciate the gravity of our monumental concerns, while we forget that if we were to become more like children our concerns might not be so monumental.

CONRAD HYERS

Youth! Stay close to the young, and a little rubs off.

ALAN JAY LERNER

Those who love the young best stay young longer.

EDGAR FRIEDENBERG

As long as I continue to hear "normal" people telling me
I am too childish, I know I'm doing just fine.

WAYNE DYER

One of the most obvious facts about grownups to a child
is that they have forgotten what it is like to be a child.

RANDELL JARRELL

All of us collect fortunes when we are children. A fortune of colors,
of lights, and darkness, of movement, of tensions. Some of us have
the fantastic chance to go back to his fortune when grown up.

INGMAR BERGMAN

So, like a forgotten fire, a childhood
can always flare up again within us.

GASTON BACHELARD

The great man is he that
does not lose his child-heart.

MENCIUS

What God is to the world, parents are to their children.

Philo

Honor your father and your mother.

Exodus 20:12

Honor your father and mother, even as you honor God,
for all three were partners in your creation.

Zohar

When I was a boy of fourteen, my father was so ignorant I could
hardly stand to have the old man around. But when I got to be
twenty-one, I was astonished at how much the old man had learned
in seven years.

Mark Twain

Remember, no matter how many candles you blow out this year,
there's one gal who will always think of you as young, strong
and handsome—your mother.

Susan D. Anderson

There's no way to be a perfect mother
and a million ways to be a good one.

JILL CHURCHILL

God could not be everywhere, therefore he made mothers.

JEWISH SAYING

Parents are often so busy with the physical rearing of children
that they miss the glory of parenthood, just as the grandeur
of the trees is lost when raking leaves.

MARCELENE COX

The best inheritance a parent can give his
children is a few minutes of his time each day.

O. A. BATTISTA

The simplest toy, one which even the youngest child
can operate, is called a grandparent.

SAM LEVENSON

**If I had known how wonderful it would be to
have grandchildren, I'd have had them first.**

Lois Wyse

Few things are more delightful than grandchildren fighting over your lap.

Doug Larson

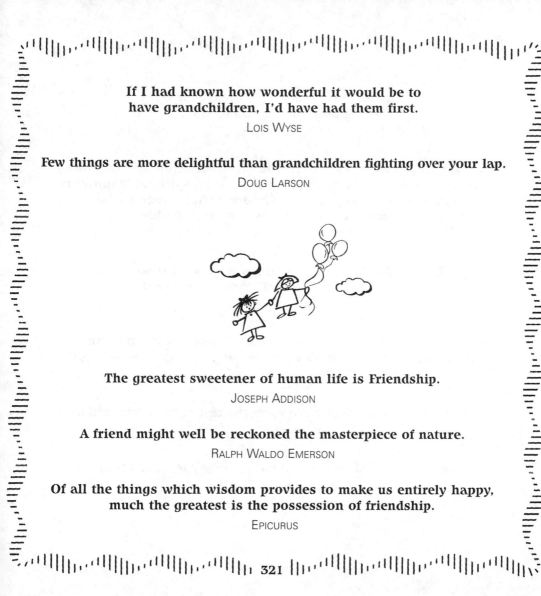

The greatest sweetener of human life is Friendship.

Joseph Addison

A friend might well be reckoned the masterpiece of nature.

Ralph Waldo Emerson

**Of all the things which wisdom provides to make us entirely happy,
much the greatest is the possession of friendship.**

Epicurus

**Friendship is the only cement that will
ever hold the world together.**

WOODROW WILSON

**The glory of friendship is not the outstretched hand, nor the kindly
smile, nor the joy of companionship; it is the spiritual inspiration
that comes to one when he discovers that someone else
believes in him and is willing to trust him.**

RALPH WALDO EMERSON

**What a great blessing is a friend with a heart so trusty
you may safely bury all your secrets in it.**

SENECA

**When a friend is in trouble, don't annoy him by asking if there is
anything you can do. Think up something appropriate and do it.**

EDGAR WATSON HOWE

A real friend is one who walks in when the rest of the world walks out.

WALTER WINCHELL

The most I can do for my friend is simply to be his friend.

HENRY DAVID THOREAU

**Friendship improves happiness, and abates misery,
by doubling our joy, and dividing our grief.**

JOSEPH ADDISON

**It is not what you give your friend, but what you are willing
to give him, that determines the quality of your friendship.**

MARY DIXON THAYER

**A friend is someone who knows all
about you and loves you just the same.**

ELBERT HUBBARD

**It is not the talking that counts between friends,
it is the never needing to say what counts.**

SHAWN GREEN

**True friendship comes when silence
between two people is comfortable.**

DAVE TYSON GENTRY

Friendship is a single soul dwelling in two bodies.

ARISTOTLE

To be a good friend remember that we are human magnets:
that like attracts like and that as we give we get.

WILFRED PETERSON

Treat your friends as you do your pictures,
and place them in their best light.

JENNIE JEROME CHURCHILL

Friendships are fragile things, and require as much care
in handling as any other fragile and precious thing.

RANDOLPH BOURNE

Every man should have a fair-sized cemetery
in which to bury the faults of his friends.

HENRY BROOKS ADAMS

Since there is nothing so well worth having as friends,
never lose a chance to make them.

FRANCESCO GUICCIARDINI

You can make more friends in two months by becoming more
interested in other people than you can in two years by trying
to get people interested in you.

DALE CARNEGIE

The only way to have a friend is to be one.

RALPH WALDO EMERSON

Friends will not only live in harmony, but in melody.

HENRY DAVID THOREAU

**It is great to have friends when one is young,
but indeed it is still more so when you are getting old.
When we are young, friends are, like everything else, a matter of
course. In the old days we know what it means to have them.**

EDVARD GRIEG

**Old friends are best. King James used to call for his old shoes;
they were the easiest for his feet.**

JOHN SELDEN

**Each of us has a spark of life inside us, and our highest endeavor
ought to be to set off that spark in one another.**

KENNY AUSUBEL

**Sometimes our light goes out but is blown into flame
by another human being. Each of us owes deepest thanks
to those who have rekindled this light.**

ALBERT SCHWEITZER

Heart

Blessed are the pure in heart, for they shall see God.

MATTHEW 5:8

The tiny flame that lights up the human heart is like a blazing torch
that comes down from heaven to light up the paths of mankind.
For in one soul are contained the hopes and feelings of all Mankind.

KAHLIL GIBRAN

Discouraged not by difficulties without, or the anguish of
ages within, the heart listens to a secret voice that whispers:
"Be not dismayed; in the future lies the Promised Land."

HELEN KELLER

When you wholeheartedly adopt a "with all your heart"
attitude and go all out with the positive principle,
you can do incredible things.

NORMAN VINCENT PEALE

When the heart of your heart opens, you can take deep pleasure
in the company of the people around you . . . When you are open
to the beauty, mystery, and grandeur of ordinary existence,
you "get it" that it always has been beautiful, mysterious,
and grand and always will be.

TIMOTHY RAY MILLER

Keep your heart open for as long as you can, as wide
as you can, for others and especially for yourself.

MORRIE SCHWARTZ

You don't have to sit on top of a mountain to discover what's
right for you. You always know in your heart what you need to do.

LIZ DOLAN

In the central place of every heart there is a recording chamber;
so long as it receives messages of beauty, hope, cheer,
and courage, so long are you young.

DOUGLAS MACARTHUR

How important is the heart! It is there that character
is formed. It alone holds the secrets of true success.

CHARLES SWINDOLL

Your heart is full of fertile seeds, waiting to sprout.

MORIHEI UESHIBA

It is the heart that makes a man rich. He is rich
according to what he is, not according to what he has.

HENRY WARD BEECHER

In the rush of daily living it's easy to forget all the remarkable people, real or fictional, who have been a part of your life. But if you just imagine they are near for a moment, you will realize that anyone who ever touched your heart is always with you, patiently waiting to emanate warmth and support whenever you remember to think of them.

BARBARA SHER

May the blessing of light be on you, light without and light within.
May the blessed sunshine shine on you and warm your heart
till it glows like a great peat fire, so that the stranger
may come and warm himself at it, and also a friend.

IRISH BLESSING

Let us labor to make the heart grow larger as we become older,
as spreading oak gives more shelter.

RICHARD JEFFRIES

If wrinkles must be written upon our brows,
let them not be written upon the heart.
The spirit should not grow old.

JAMES A. GARFIELD

Great thoughts come from the heart.

LUC DE CLAPIERS

The best and most beautiful things in the world cannot be seen or even touched. They must be felt with the heart.

HELEN KELLER

Trust your intuitive heart.

RICHARD CARLSON

What the heart knows today, the head will understand tomorrow.

JAMES STEPHENS

It is only with the heart that one can see rightly; what is essential is invisible to the eye.

ANTOINE DE SAINT-EXUPÉRY

A light heart lives long.

WILLIAM SHAKESPEARE

**The one important thing I have learned over the years is the difference
between taking one's work seriously and taking one's self seriously.
The first is imperative and the second is disastrous.**

MARGOT FONTEYN

**Man, unlike the animal, has never learned
that the sole purpose of life is to enjoy it.**

SAMUEL BUTLER

There is no cure for birth or death save to enjoy the interval.

GEORGE SANTAYANA

Life's better when it's fun. Boy, that's deep, isn't it?

KEVIN COSTNER

**When a man is gloomy, everything seems to go wrong;
when he is cheerful, everything seems right!**

PROVERBS 15:15

**An ounce of cheerfulness is worth a
pound of sadness to serve God with.**

THOMAS FULLER

**Years back someone said cod liver oil was the cure-all!
Cheerfulness is more palliative and with no unpleasant aftertaste.**

SR. MARY CHRISTELLE MACALUSO

**Cheerfulness keeps up a kind of daylight in the mind,
filling it with a steady and perpetual serenity.**

JOSEPH ADDISON

**The highest wisdom is continual cheerfulness; such a state,
like the region above the moon, is always clear and serene.**

MONTAIGNE

**Let us be of good cheer, remembering that misfortunes
hardest to bear are those which never come.**

JAMES RUSSELL LOWELL

Burdens become light when cheerfully borne.

OVID

**A happy woman is one who has no cares at all; a cheerful woman
is one who has cares but doesn't let them get her down.**

BEVERLY SILLS

Even if we can't be happy
we must always be cheerful.

IRVING KRISTOL

Nature intended you to be the fountain-spring
of cheerfulness and social life,
and not the mountain of despair and melancholy.

SIR ARTHUR HELPS

You find yourself refreshed by the presence
of cheerful people. Why not make an earnest effort
to confer that pleasure on others?
Half the battle is gained if you never allow yourself
to say anything gloomy.

LYDIA MARIA CHILD

Cheerfulness is contagious, but don't wait
to catch it from others. Be a carrier.

ANONYMOUS

If God came in and said, "I want you to be happy for the
rest of your life," what would you do?

BERNIE SIEGEL

True happiness is to understand our duties toward God and man;
to enjoy the present, without anxious dependence on the future;
not to amuse ourselves with either hopes or fears, but to rest satisfied
with what we have, which is abundantly sufficient.

SENECA

Many people think that if they were only in some other place, or had
some other job, they would be happy. Well, that is doubtful. So get
as much happiness out of what you are doing as you can and don't
put off being happy until some future date.

DALE CARNEGIE

You're happiest while you're making the greatest contribution.

ROBERT F. KENNEDY

The happiest and most contented people are those who
each day perform to make the best of their abilities.

ALFRED A. MONTAPERT

None but those who are happy in themselves can make others so.

WILLIAM HAZLITT

Do you want a world with . . . more joy and happiness? Then find your own joy and happiness and contribute to the joy and happiness of others.

BO LOZOFF

One thing I know; the only ones among you who will be really happy are those who will have sought and found how to serve.

ALBERT SCHWEITZER

Happiness is a perfume which you cannot pour on someone without getting some on yourself.

RALPH WALDO EMERSON

Remember that happiness is as contagious as gloom. It should be the first duty of those who are happy to let others know of their gladness.

MAURICE MAETERLINCK

Those who are happiest are those who do the most for others.

BOOKER T. WASHINGTON

Make people happy and there will not be half the quarreling, or a tenth part of the wickedness there now is.

LYDIA MARIA CHILD

Lead the life that will make you kindly and friendly to everyone about you, and you will be surprised what a happy life you will lead.

CHARLES SCHWAB

If you want to be happy, set yourself a goal that commands your thoughts, liberates your energy, and inspires your hopes. Happiness is within you. It comes from doing some certain thing into which you can put all your thought and energy. If you want to be happy, get enthusiastic about something.

DALE CARNEGIE

Happiness lies in the joy of achievement and the thrill of creative effort.

FRANKLIN D. ROOSEVELT

The way to happiness: keep your heart free from hate, your mind from worry. Live simply, expect little, give much. Fill your life with love. Scatter sunshine. Forget self, think of others. Do as you would be done by. Try this for a week and you will be surprised.

NORMAN VINCENT PEALE

The happiness of life is made up of minute fractions—the little, soon-forgotten charities of a kiss or smile, a kind look, a heartfelt compliment, and the countless infinitesimals of pleasurable and genial feeling.

SAMUEL TAYLOR COLERIDGE

**A happy life is made up of little things . . .
a gift sent, a letter written, a call made, a recommendation given,
transportation provided, a cake made, a book lent, a check sent.**

CAROL HOLMES

**Do not worry; eat three square meals a day; say your prayers;
be courteous to your creditors; keep your digestion good; exercise;
go slow and easy. Maybe there are other things your special case
requires to make you happy, but my friend, these I reckon
will give you a good life.**

ABRAHAM LINCOLN

**The secret of happiness is this: Let your interests be as wide as possible,
and let your reactions to the things and persons that interest you
be as far as possible friendly rather than hostile.**

BERTRAND RUSSELL

**The secret of happiness is not in doing what one likes,
but in liking what one does.**

J. M. BARRIE

**The secret of happiness is to count your blessings
while others are adding up their troubles.**

WILLIAM PENN

The secret of happiness is to count your
blessings—not your birthdays.

SHANNON ROSE

To be without some of the things you want
is an indispensable part of happiness.

BERTRAND RUSSELL

It is not how much we have, but how
much we enjoy, that makes happiness.

CHARLES SPURGEON

Before strongly desiring anything,
we should look carefully into the happiness of its present owner.

LA ROCHEFOUCAULD

We have all been placed on this earth to discover our own path,
and we will never be happy if we live someone else's idea of life.

JAMES VAN PRAAGH

The grand essentials to happiness in this life are something
to do, something to love, and something to hope for.

JOSEPH ADDISON

But what is happiness except the simple harmony
between a man and the life he leads.

ALBERT CAMUS

We all have 100% to deal with in our lives: 10% is important,
90% unimportant. The secret to a happy, productive life
is to deal with the 10% and let the 90% slip.

SALLI RASBERRY AND PADI SELWYN

With a little discipline and regular self-checks, you can learn to do
one thing at a time. And do it better. And be happier doing it.

ELAINE ST. JAMES

I've been riding the carousel in Central Park since I was five years old . . .
If I'm very depressed or if something's bothering me today, my husband,
Larry, and I go back to the park. We get on the carousel horse and we
start riding, and I start singing at the top of my lungs. It is pure and
absolute joy and happiness.

EDA LeSHAN

It's never too late to have a happy childhood.

ANONYMOUS

Life holds so much, so much to be happy about always.
Most people ask for happiness on condition.
Happiness can be felt only if you don't set any conditions.

ARTUR RUBENSTEIN

Happiness is the spiritual experience of living
every minute with love, grace, and gratitude.

DENIS WAITLEY

Better to be happy than wise.

JOHN HEYWOOD

Happiness is a butterfly, which, when pursued, is always just beyond
your grasp, but which, if you will sit down quietly, may alight upon you.

NATHANIEL HAWTHORNE

Your success and happiness lie in you. Resolve to keep happy,
and your joy and you shall form an invisible host against difficulties.

HELEN KELLER

Remember that happiness is a way of travel, not a destination.

ROY GOODMAN

When ill luck besets us, to ease the tension we have only to
remember that happiness is relative. The next time you are tempted
to grumble about what has happened to you, why not pause and
be glad that it is no worse than it is?

DALE CARNEGIE

When one door of happiness closes, another opens; but often we look so long at the closed door that we do not see the one which has been opened for us.

HELEN KELLER

Many search for happiness as we look
for a hat we wear on our heads.

NIKOLAUS LENUS

I have found that most people are about as happy
as they make up their minds to be.

ABRAHAM LINCOLN

It is the happiness that comes from within that is lasting and fulfilling.

LEDDY SCHMELIGH

Each person on this planet is inherently, intrinsically capable
of attaining "dizzying heights" of happiness and fulfillment.

WAYNE DYER

The ingredients of happiness are so simple that they can be counted
on one hand. Happiness comes from within, and rests most securely
on simple goodness and clear conscience.

WILLIAM OGDEN

We are never so happy nor so unhappy as we imagine.
LA ROCHEFOUCAULD

You have to believe in happiness, or happiness never comes.
DOUGLAS MALLOCH

It is a man's proper business to seek happiness and avoid misery.
JOHN LOCKE

The best way to secure future happiness
is to be as happy as is rightfully possible today.
CHARLES ELIOT

Why should we refuse the happiness this hour gives us,
because some other hour might take it away?
JOHN OLIVER HOBBES

At the end of our time on earth, if we have lived
fully, we will not be able to say, "I was always happy."
Hopefully, we will be able to say, "I have experienced a lifetime
of real moments, and many of them were happy moments."
BARBARA DEANGELIS

Cherish all your happy moments; they make a fine cushion for old age.
BOOTH TARKINGTON

Happiness is the meaning and the purpose of life,
the whole aim and end of human existence.

ARISTOTLE

The time to be happy is now. The place to be happy is here.

ROBERT G. INGERSOLL

Happiness and love are just a choice away.

LEO BUSCAGLIA

Our happiness depends on the habit of mind we cultivate.
So practice happy thinking every day. Cultivate the merry heart,
develop the happiness habit, and life will become a continual feast.

NORMAN VINCENT PEALE

Humor is the healthy way of feeling "distance" between one's self
and the problem, a way of standing off and looking
at one's problems with perspective.

ROLLO MAY

Humor has great power to heal on an emotional level.
You can't hold anger, you can't hold fear,
you can't hold hurt while you're laughing.

STEVE BHAERMAN
(A.K.A. SWAMI BEYONDANANDA)

Humor enables one to live in the midst of
tragic events without becoming a tragic figure.

E. T. "CY" EBERHART

There is no defense against adverse fortune which is
so effectual as an habitual sense of humor.

THOMAS HIGGINSON

Humor is our way of defending ourselves from life's
absurdities by thinking absurdly about them.

LEWIS MUMFORD

Common sense and a sense of humor are the same thing, moving at
different speeds. A sense of humor is just common sense, dancing.

CLIVE JAMES

There is always something to chuckle about. Sometimes we see it.
Sometimes . . . we don't. Still, the world is filled with humor.
It is there when we are happy and it is there to cheer us up when we are not.

ALLEN KLEIN

Joy is the most infallible sign of the Presence of God.

TEILHARD DE CHARDIN

Listen to the clues. The next time you feel real joy, stop and think. Pay attention. Because joy is the universe's way of knocking on your mind's door. Hello in there. Is anyone home? Can I leave a message? Yes? Good! The message is that you are happy, and that means that you are in touch with your purpose.

STEVE CHANDLER

Joy of life seems to me to arise from a sense of being where one belongs . . . of being foursquare with the life we have chosen. All the discontented people I know are trying sedulously to be something they are not, to do something they cannot do.

DAVID GRAYSON

When we align our thoughts, emotions, and actions with the highest part of ourselves, we are filled with enthusiasm, purpose, and meaning. . . . We are joyously and intimately engaged with our world. This is the experience of authentic power.

GARY ZUKAV

We have a tendency to obscure the forest of simple joys
with the trees of problems.

CHRISTIANE COLLANGE

People need joy quite as much as clothing. Some of them need it far more.

MARGARET COLLIER GRAHAM

When large numbers of people share their joy in common, the
happiness of each is greater because each adds fuel to the other's flame.

SAINT AUGUSTINE

Joys divided are increased.

JOSIAH GILBERT HOLLAND

You increase your joy by increasing the pure joy of others.

TORKOM SARAYDARIAN

Joy increases as you give it, and diminishes as you try
to keep it for yourself. In giving it, you will accumulate
a deposit of joy greater than you ever believed possible.

NORMAN VINCENT PEALE

As you express joy, you draw it out of those you meet,
creating joyful people and joyful events. The greater
the joy you express, the more joy you experience.

ARNOLD PATENT

When we feel joyful, euphoric, happy, we are more open to life, more capable of seeing things clearly and handling daily tensions.

LEO BUSCAGLIA

If we could learn how to balance rest against effort, calmness against strain, quiet against turmoil, we would assure ourselves of joy in living and psychological health for life.

JOSEPHINE RATHBONE

Simplicity, clarity, singleness: these are the attributes that give our lives power and vividness and joy.

RICHARD HALLOWAY

Joy is not in things; it is in us.

RICHARD WAGNER

Joy is the feeling of grinning on the inside.

MELBA COLGROVE

Joy is the will which labors, which overcomes obstacles, which knows triumph.

WILLIAM BUTLER YEATS

It is in the compelling zest of high adventure and of victory, and in creative action, that man finds his supreme joy.

ANTOINE DE SAINT-EXUPÉRY

I believe humans were born to have joy and to have it more abundantly; that the birthright of everyone is loving, caring, sharing, and abundance.

PETER MCWILLIAMS AND JOHN-ROGER

Joy is your birthright.

SARAH BAN BREATHNACH

Blessed are the joymakers.

NATHANIEL PARKER WILLIS

Laughter is the closest thing to the grace of God.

KARL BARTH

How to make God laugh: Tell him your future plans.

WOODY ALLEN

God is a comedian whose audience is afraid to laugh.

H. L. MENCKEN

Although a lot can be learned from adversity,
most of the same lessons can be learned
through laughter and joy.

PETER McWILLIAMS

So when you're lonely or sad or bad or blue remember
where laughter's hiding . . . it's hiding inside of YOU!

DAVID SALTZMAN

Against the assault of laughter nothing can stand.

MARK TWAIN

In every job, relationship, or life situation there is inevitably some
turbulence. Learn to laugh at it. It is part of what you do and who you are.

ALLEN KLEIN

Laughter puts your brain, your central nervous system
and your whole being into a state of free play.

MAX EASTMAN

Laughing deeply is living deeply.

MILAN KUNDERA

It has always seemed to me that hearty laughter is
a good way to jog internally without having to go outdoors.

NORMAN COUSINS

A good belly laugh is like taking
your liver for a horseback ride.

BONNY CLARK

He laughs best whose laugh lasts.

LAURENCE J. PETER

Shared laughter is like throwing open the shutters in
a gloomy room and letting in fresh air and sunshine.

LILA GREEN

Laughter is the sun that drives winter from the human race.

VICTOR HUGO

Shared laughter is love made audible.

IZZY GESELL

A good laugh helps us recognize how ridiculous it is
to get excited about matters that are often trivial. . . .

ARTHUR ASA BERGER

Laughter is the brush that sweeps
away the cobwebs of the heart.

MORT WALKER

When we can laugh through out tears, we are being given a powerful message. Things may be bad, but they cannot be all that bad.

ALLEN KLEIN

The child in you, like all children, loves to laugh, to be around people who can laugh at themselves and life. Children instinctively know that the more laughter we have in our lives, the better.

WAYNE DYER

Laughter is a gift everyone should open.

GENE MITCHENER

In the true man there is a child concealed—who wants to play.

FRIEDRICH NIETZSCHE

Play keeps us vital and alive. It gives us an enthusiasm for life that is irreplaceable. Without it, life just doesn't taste good.

LUCIA CAPACCHIONE

It's good to play, and you must keep in practice.

JERRY SEINFELD

The supreme accomplishment is to blur the line between work and play.

ARNOLD TOYNBEE

A little work, a little play,
To keep us going—and so, good-day!

GEORGE DU MAURIER

Get out of bed forcing a smile. You may not smile because you
are cheerful; but if you will force yourself to smile
you'll . . . be cheerful because you smile.

KENNETH GOODE

He who smiles rather than rages is always the stronger.

JAPANESE PROVERB

Every time a man smiles, and much more when
he laughs, it adds something to his fragment of life.

LAURENCE STERNE

What sunshine is to flowers, smiles are to humanity.
They are but trifles, to be sure; but, scattered along life's
pathway, the good they do is inconceivable.

JOSEPH ADDISON

√ It's easy enough to be pleasant when everything goes like a song,
but the man who is worthwhile, is the man who can smile,
when everything goes dead wrong.

ANONYMOUS

√ If you have made another person on this earth smile,
your life has been worthwhile.

SR. MARY CHRISTELLE MACALUSO

Wrinkles should merely indicate where smiles have been.

MARK TWAIN

Of all the things you wear, your expression is the most important.

JANET LANE

It is only through love that we can attain to communion with God.
All living knowledge of God rest upon this foundation:
that we experience Him in our lives as Will-to-love.

ALBERT SCHWEITZER

One word frees us of all the weight and pain
of life: That word is love.

SOPHOCLES

It makes no difference how deeply seated may be the trouble; how
hopeless the outlook; how muddled the tangle; how great the mistake.
A sufficient realization of love will dissolve it all. If only you could love
enough you would be the happiest and most powerful being in the world.

EMMET FOX

Love is the master key which opens the gates of happiness.

OLIVER WENDELL HOLMES, SR.

There is only one happiness in life, to love and be loved.

GEORGE SAND

Let no one who loves be called unhappy.
Even love unreturned has its rainbow.

J. M. BARRIE

What a grand thing, to be loved! What a grander thing still, to love!

VICTOR HUGO

To love and be loved is to feel the sun from both sides.

DAVID VISCOTT

Love . . . binds everything together in perfect harmony.

COLOSSIANS 3:14

For love . . . is the blood of life, the power of reunion in the separated.

PAUL TILLICH

It is this intangible thing, love in many forms, which enters into every
therapeutic relationship. . . . And it is an element which binds and
heals, which comforts and restores, which works what we have to
call—for now—miracles.

KARL MENNINGER

This is the miracle that happens every time to those
who really love; the more they give, the more they possess.

RAINER MARIA RILKE

The one thing we can never get enough of is love.
And the one thing we never give enough of is love.

HENRY MILLER

Love sought is good, but given unsought is better.

WILLIAM SHAKESPEARE

Don't shut love out of your life by saying it's impossible to find time.
The quickest way to receive love is to give; the fastest way to lose love
is to hold it too tightly; and the best way to keep love is to give it wings.

BRIAN DYSON

The love we give away is the only one we keep.

ELBERT HUBBARD

If you would be loved, love and be lovable.

BENJAMIN FRANKLIN

The issue is not so much being loved but being loving, which leads
to the same wonderful feeling you experience when someone loves you.

CAROL PEARSON

Everybody forgets the basic thing: people are
not going to love you unless you love them.

PAT CARROLL

A loving person lives in a loving world. A hostile person
lives in a hostile world: everyone you meet is your mirror.

KEN KEYES, JR.

Nine times out of ten, when you extend your arms to someone,
they will step in, because basically they need precisely what you need.

LEO BUSCAGLIA

Love your enemies because they bring out the best in you.

FRIEDRICH NIETZSCHE

Tolerance and celebration of individual
differences is the fire that fuels lasting love.

TOM HANNAH

Do not waste time bothering whether you "love" your
neighbor; act as if you did. As soon as we do this we find
one of the great secrets. When you are behaving as if you
loved someone, you will presently come to love him.

C. S. LEWIS

Thou shalt love thy neighbor as thyself.

LEVITICUS 19:18

Love is a force that connects us to every strand of the universe, an unconditional state that characterizes human nature, a form of knowledge that is always there for us if only we can open ourselves to it.

EMILY HILBURN SELL

When we connect with ourselves in love, we can connect with others and the planet in love.

RATTANA HETZEL

Choose to be a love-finder rather than a faultfinder.

GERALD JAMPOLSKY

If you judge people, you have no time to love them.

MOTHER TERESA

Someday, after we have mastered the winds, the waves, the tide and gravity, we shall harness for God the energies of love. Then, for the second time in the history of the world, man will have discovered fire.

TEILHARD DE CHARDIN

Love keeps the cold out better than a cloak.

HENRY WADSWORTH LONGFELLOW

In the coldest February, as in every other month in every other year, the best thing to hold on to in this world is each other.

LINDA ELLERBEE

True love always brings joy to ourself and to the one we love. If our love does not bring joy to both of us, it is not true love.

THICH NHAT HANH

True love comes quietly, without banners or flashing lights. If you hear bells, get your ears checked.

ERICH SEGAL

True love is night jasmine, a diamond in darkness, the heartbeat no cardiologist has ever heard. It is the most common of miracles, fashioned of fleecy clouds—a handful of stars tossed into the night sky.

JIM BISHOP

The essence of love is kindness.

ROBERT LOUIS STEVENSON

Love is what we were born with. Fear is what we learned here.

MARIANNE WILLIAMSON

Love is letting go of fear.

GERALD JAMPOLSKY

Love is much nicer to be in than an automobile accident, a tight girdle, a higher tax bracket, or a holding pattern over Philadelphia.

JUDITH VIORST

The Eskimos had fifty-two names for snow because it was important to them; there ought to be as many for love.

MARGARET ATWOOD

Every single one of us can do things that no one else can do— can love things that no one else can love . . . We are like violins. We can be used for doorstops, or we can make music.

BARBARA SHER

But some emotions don't make a lot of noise. It's hard to hear pride. Caring is real faint—like a heartbeat. And pure love— why, some days it's so quiet, you don't even know it's there.

ERMA BOMBECK

Love is not what we become but who we already are.

STEPHEN LEVINE

Ultimately, love is self-approval.

SONDRA RAY

Love is, above all, the gift of oneself.

JEAN ANOUILH

You must love yourself before you love another. By accepting yourself and fully being what you are . . . your simple presence can make others happy.

JANE ROBERTS

It is not what we do, it is how much love we put in the doing.

MOTHER TERESA

Forget the resolutions. Forget control and discipline . . . too much work. Instead try experimenting. Go in search of something to fall in love with . . . something about yourself, your career, your spouse.

DALE DAUTEN

Find something you love to do and you'll never have to work a day in your life.

HARVEY MACKAY

You will find, as you look back upon your life, that the moments when you really lived are the moments when you have done things in the spirit of love.

HENRY DRUMMOND

We are most alive when we're in love.

JOHN UPDIKE

In our life there is a single color, as on an artist's palette,
which provides the meaning of life and art. It is the color of love.

MARC CHAGALL

Life is a flower of which love is the honey.

VICTOR HUGO

No one who has ever brought up a child can doubt for a moment
that love is literally the life-giving fluid of human existence.

SMILEY BLANTON

Anything will give up its secrets if you love it enough. Not only have I
found that when I talk to the little flower or to the little peanut they
will give up their secrets, but I have found that when I silently commune
with people they give up their secrets also—if you love them enough.

GEORGE WASHINGTON CARVER

A five-word sentence that could change the world tomorrow is
"What would love do now?"

NEALE DONALD WALSCH

Do not seek perfection in a changing world.
Instead, perfect your love.

MASTER SENGSTAN

Every day we are offered new means for learning and growing in love.

LEO BUSCAGLIA

Spend a moment, every day, thinking of someone to love.

RICHARD CARLSON

Ultimately love is everything.

M. SCOTT PECK

What the world really needs is more love and less paperwork.

PEARL BAILEY

Love doesn't make the world go 'round.
Love is what makes the ride worthwhile.

FRANKLIN P. JONES

Love is how you stay alive, even after you are gone.

MORRIE SCHWARTZ

God's miracles are to be found in nature itself;
the wind and waves, the wood that becomes a tree—all of these
are explained biologically, but behind them is the hand of God.

RONALD REAGAN

When I first open my eyes upon the morning meadows
and look out upon the beautiful world, I thank God I am alive.

RALPH WALDO EMERSON

If you wish to know the divine, feel the wind
on your face and the warm sun on your hand.

EIDO TAI SHIMANO ROSHI

The radiance in some places is so great as to be fairly dazzling . . .
every crystal, every flower a window opening into heaven,
a mirror reflecting the Creator.

JOHN MUIR

Nature is too thin a screen; the glory of
the omnipresent God bursts through everywhere.

RALPH WALDO EMERSON

I believe a leaf of grass is no less than the journey-work of the stars.

WALT WHITMAN

Look deep, deep into nature, and then you will
understand everything better.

ALBERT EINSTEIN

Come forth into the light of things. Let nature be your teacher.

WILLIAM WORDSWORTH

If you watch how nature deals with adversity,
continually renewing itself, you can't help but learn.

BERNIE SIEGEL

Rivers and rocks and trees have always been talking to us,
but we've forgotten how to listen.

MICHAEL ROADS

Contemplate the workings of this world. . . . Study how water flows in a
valley stream, smoothly and freely between the rocks . . . Everything—
even mountains, rivers, plants, and trees—should be your teacher.

MORIHEI UESHIBA

Speak to the earth, and it shall teach thee.

JOB 12:8

Adopt the pace of nature: her secret is patience.

RALPH WALDO EMERSON

Climb the mountains and get their good tidings: Nature's peace
will flow into you as sunshine into flowers, the winds will
blow their freshness into you, and the storms,
their energy and cares will drop off like autumn leaves.

JOHN MUIR

Nature tops the list of potent tranquilizers and stress reducers. The
mere sound of moving water has been shown to lower blood pressure.

PATCH ADAMS

The sun—my almighty physician.

THOMAS JEFFERSON

Nature uses only the longest threads to weave her patterns, so each
small piece of her fabric reveals the organization of the entire tapestry.

RICHARD FEYNMAN

The finest workers in stone are not copper or steel tools,
but the gentle touches of air and water working at their leisure
with a liberal allowance of time.

HENRY DAVID THOREAU

To the dull mind all nature is leaden. To the illumined
mind the whole world burns and sparkles with light.

RALPH WALDO EMERSON

The beauty of the world and the orderly arrangement of everything celestial makes us confess that there is an excellent and eternal nature, which ought to be worshiped and admired by all mankind.

CICERO

In all things of nature there is something of the marvelous.

ARISTOTLE

The sun gives us light, but the moon provides inspiration.
If you look at the sun without shielding your eyes, you'll go blind.
If you look at the moon without covering your eyes, you'll become a poet.

SERGE BOUCHARD

The world is full of poetry. The air is living with its spirit; and the waves dance to the music of its melodies, and sparkle in its brightness.

PERCIVAL

The sky is the daily bread of the eyes.

RALPH WALSO EMERSON

My heart leaps up when I behold a rainbow in the sky.

WILLIAM WORDSWORTH

The bluebird carries the sky on his back.

HENRY DAVID THOREAU

The clearest way into the Universe is through a forest wilderness.

JOHN MUIR

We lose our souls if we lose the experience of the forest, the
butterflies, the song of the birds, if we can't see the stars at night.

THOMAS BERRY

Forget not that the earth delights to feel your bare feet
and the winds long to play with your hair.

KAHLIL GIBRAN

As long as the Earth can make a spring every year, I can.
As long as the Earth can flower and produce nurturing fruit, I can,
because I'm the Earth. I won't give up until the Earth gives up.

ALICE WALKER

The creation of a thousand forests is in one acorn.

RALPH WALDO EMERSON

I never knew how soothing trees are—many trees
and patches of open sunlight, and tree presences;
it is almost like having another being.

D. H. LAWRENCE

Nature is saturated with deity.

RALPH WALDO EMERSON

Our Lord has written the promise of resurrection,
not in books alone but in every leaf of springtime.

MARTIN LUTHER

The nicest thing about the promise of spring
is that sooner or later she'll have to keep it.

MARK BELTAIRE

Spring is nature's way of saying, "Let's party!"

ROBIN WILLIAMS

It was one of those perfect summer days—the sun was shining, a breeze
was blowing, the birds were singing, and the lawnmower was broken.

JAMES DENT

Nobody sees a flower—really—it is so small it takes time—
we haven't time—and to see takes time, like to have a friend takes time.

GEORGIA O'KEEFFE

Consider the lilics of the field, how they grow; they neither toil
nor spin; yet I tell you, even Solomon in all his glory was not
arrayed like one of these.

MATTHEW 6:28

The Amen! of Nature is always a flower.

OLIVER WENDELL HOLMES, SR.

Next time a sunrise steals your breath or a meadow of flowers leave you speechless, remain that way. Say nothing, and listen as heaven whispers, "Do you like it? I did it just for you."

MAX LUCADO

Every flower is a soul blossoming in Nature.

GÉRARD DE NERVAL

Flowers always make people better, happier, and more helpful; they are sunshine, food, and medicine to the soul.

LUTHER BURBANK

Earth laughs in flowers.

RALPH WALDO EMERSON

God Almighty first planted a garden. And indeed it is the purest of human pleasures.

FRANCIS BACON

Pleasure for an hour, a bottle of wine; pleasure for a year, marriage; pleasure for a lifetime, a garden.

CHINESE SAYING

The kiss of sun for pardon,
The song of the birds for mirth
One is nearer God's Heart in a garden
Than anywhere else on earth.

DOROTHY GURNEY

All gardeners live in beautiful places because they make them so.

JOSEPH JOUBERT

All gardening is landscape painting.

ALEXANDER POPE

What is a weed? A plant whose virtues have not yet been discovered.

RALPH WALDO EMERSON

For many years I was self-appointed inspector of snowstorms and rainstorms, and did my duty faithfully, though I never received one cent for it.

HENRY DAVID THOREAU

The next time it begins to rain . . . lie down on your belly, nestle your chin into the grass, and get a frog's-eye view of how raindrops fall . . . The sight of hundreds of blades of grass bowing down and popping back up like piano keys strikes me as one of the merriest sights in the world.

MALCOLM MARGOLIN

Sunshine is delicious, rain is refreshing, wind braces us up, snow is exhilarating; there is really no such thing as bad weather, only different kinds of good weather.

JOHN RUSKIN

Don't knock the weather; nine-tenths of the people couldn't start a conversation if it didn't change once in a while.

KIN HUBBARD

After rain comes fair weather.

JAMES HOWELL

Weather means more when you have a garden. There's nothing like listening to a shower and thinking how it is soaking in around your green beans.

MARCELENE COX

**This is the day the Lord had made.
We will rejoice and be glad in it.**

PSALMS 118:24

**I have always been delighted at the prospect of a new day,
a fresh try, one more start, with perhaps a bit of magic
waiting somewhere behind the morning.**

J. B. PRIESTLY

**Whether one is twenty, forty, or sixty; whether one has succeeded,
failed or just muddled along; whether yesterday was full of sun or storm,
or one of those dull days with no weather at all, life begins each morning!**

LEIGH MITCHELL HODGES

**Today a new sun rises for me; everything lives,
everything is animated, everything seems to speak
to me of my passion, everything invites me to cherish it.**

ANNE DE LENCLOS

**Every new day begins with possibilities. It's up to us
to fill it with the things that move us toward progress and peace.**

RONALD REAGAN

I love the challenge of starting at zero every day
and seeing how much I can accomplish.

MARTHA STEWART

Thank God ever morning when you get up that you have
something to do which must be done, whether you like it or not.

CHARLES KINGSLEY

Today is a new day. You will get out of it just what you put into it . . .
If you have made mistakes, even serious mistakes, there is always another
chance for you. . . . for this thing that we call "failure"
is not the falling down, but the staying down.

MARY PICKFORD

Finish each day and be done with it. You have done what you could;
some blunders and absurdities have crept in; forget them as soon as you
can. Tomorrow is a new day; you shall begin it serenely and with too
high a spirit to be encumbered with your old nonsense.

RALPH WALDO EMERSON

Live your life each day as you would climb a mountain.
An occasional glance toward the summit keeps the goal in mind,
but many beautiful scenes are to be observed from each new vantage point.
Climb slowly, steadily, enjoying each passing moment; and the view from
the summit will serve as a fitting climax for the journey.

HAROLD B. MELCHART

Nothing is worth more than this day.

GOETHE

Write it on your heart that every day is the best day in the year.

RALPH WALDO EMERSON

Normal day, let me be aware of the treasure you are.
Let me learn from you, love you, bless you before you depart.
Let me not pass you by in quest of some rare and perfect tomorrow.

MARY JEAN IRON

Yesterday is not ours to recover, but tomorrow is ours to win or lose.

LYNDON B. JOHNSON

When all else is lost, the future still remains.

CHRISTIAN BOVEE

When I look at the future, it's so bright, it burns my eyes.

OPRAH WINFREY

Pets

Cats   Dogs

Peace

Positive Thoughts

Time spent with cats is never wasted.

COLETTE

There are two means of refuge from the miseries of life: music and cats.

ALBERT SCHWEITZER

You can't look at a sleeping cat and be tense.

JANE PAULEY

**It is impossible to keep a straight face
in the presence of one or more kittens.**

CYNTHIA E. VARNADO

**Dogs come when they're called;
cats take a message and get back to you.**

MARY BLY

**Cats are smarter than dogs. You can't
get eight cats to pull a sled through snow.**

JEFF VALDEZ

Cats seem to go on the principle that it
never does any harm to ask for what you want.

JOSEPH WOOD KRUTCH

Cats are angels with fur.

SARK

Whoever said you can't buy happiness forgot about little puppies.

GENE HILL

There is no psychiatrist in the world like a puppy licking your face.

BERN WILLIAMS

Know thyself. Don't accept your dog's admiration
as conclusive evidence that you are wonderful.

ANN LANDERS

Dogs are not our whole life, but they make our lives whole.

ROGER CARAS

Living with a dog is one way to retain something of a child's spirit.

MICHAEL ROSEN

**A dog is the only thing on earth
that loves you more than he loves himself.**

JOSH BILLINGS

**The greatest pleasure of a dog is that you may make a fool
of yourself with him, and not only will he not scold you,
but he will make a fool of himself, too.**

SAMUEL BUTLER

The dog is the god of frolic.

HENRY WARD BEECHER

**I wonder if other dogs think poodles
are members of a weird religious cult.**

RITA RUDNER

**I have always thought of a dog lover
as a dog that was in love with another dog.**

JAMES THURBER

A dog wags its tail with its heart.

MARTIN BUXBAUM

Dogs laugh, but they laugh with their tails.

MAX EASTMAN

Money will buy a pretty good dog
but it won't buy the wag of his tail.

JOSH BILLINGS

No matter how little money and how few
possessions you own, having a dog makes you rich.

LOUIS SABIN

Peace is the first thing the angels sang. Peace is the mark of the sons
of God. Peace is the nurse of love. Peace is the mother of unity.
Peace is the rest of blessed souls. Peace is the dwelling place of eternity.

LEO THE GREAT

Peace is a daily, a weekly, a monthly process, gradually changing opinions,
slowly eroding old barriers, quietly building new structures. And however
undramatic the pursuit of peace, the pursuit must go on.

JOHN F. KENNEDY

Choose to experience peace rather than conflict.

GERALD JAMPOLSKY

You don't have to have fought in a war to love peace.

GERALDINE FERRARO

**War is an invention of the human mind.
The human mind can invent peace.**

NORMAN COUSINS

**I think that people want peace so much that one of these days
governments had better get out of their way and let them have it.**

DWIGHT D. EISENHOWER

**If we have no peace, it is because we have forgotten
that we belong to each other.**

MOTHER TERESA

**Until he extends his circle of compassion to
all living things, man will not find peace.**

ALBERT SCHWEITZER

**It isn't enough to talk about peace; one must believe in it.
And it isn't enough to believe in it; one must work at it.**

ELEANOR ROOSEVELT

Before it's too late, and time is running out, let us turn from trust
in the chain reactions of exploding atoms to faith of the chain
reaction of God's love. Love—love of God and fellow men.
That is God's formula for peace.

RICHARD CARDINAL CUSHING

The more we sweat in peace the less we bleed in war.

VIJAYA LAKSHMI PANDIT

It is understanding that gives us an ability to have peace. When
we understand the other fellow's viewpoint, and he understands
ours, then we can sit down and work out our differences.

HARRY S TRUMAN

It takes two to make peace.

JOHN F. KENNEDY

We merely want to live in peace with all the world,
to trade with them, to commune with them, to learn from their
culture as they may learn from ours, so that the products of our
toil may be used for our schools and our roads and our churches
and not for guns and planes and tanks and ships of war.

DWIGHT D. EISENHOWER

The place to improve the world is first
in one's own heart and head and hands.

ROBERT PERSIG

**If we have not peace within ourselves, it is
in vain to seek it from outward sources.**

LA ROCHEFOUCAULD

**The only way to bring peace to the earth
is to learn to make our own life peaceful.**

THE BUDDHA

Peace, like charity, begins at home.

FRANKLIN D. ROOSEVELT

**May you have warmth in your igloo, oil in your lamp,
and peace in your heart.**

ESKIMO PROVERB

Positive thoughts (joy, happiness, fulfillment, achievement, worthiness)
have positive results (enthusiasm, calm, well-being, ease, energy, love).
Negative thoughts (judgment, unworthiness, mistrust, resentment, fear)
produce negative results (tension, anxiety, alienation, anger, fatigue).

PETER McWILLIAMS AND JOHN-ROGER

Could we change our attitude, we should not only see life differently,
but life itself would come to be different. Life would undergo a change of
appearance because we ourselves had undergone a change in attitude.

KATHERINE MANSFIELD

Life is a mirror and will reflect back to the thinker what he thinks into it.

ERNEST HOLMES

Our thoughts and imaginations are the only real limits to our possibilities.

ORISON S. MARDEN

It is the mind that maketh good of ill, that maketh wretch or happy,
rich or poor.

EDMUND SPENSER

Most of us can, as we choose, make of this
world either a palace or a prison.

SIR JOHN LUBBOCK

We are each gifted in a unique and important way. It is our
privilege and our adventure to discover our own special light.

MARY DUNBAR

Before a painter puts a brush to his canvas he sees his picture
mentally. . . . If you think of yourself in terms of a painting, what do
you see? . . . Is the picture one you think worth painting? . . . You
create yourself in the image you hold in your mind.

THOMAS DREIER

We cannot tell what may happen to us in the strange medley of life.
But we can decide what happens in us—how we take it,
what we do with it—and that is what really counts in the end.

JOSEPH NEWTON

Get into the habit of looking for the silver lining of the cloud, and,
when you have found it, continue to look at it, rather than at the
leaden gray in the middle. It will help you over many hard places.

A. A. WILLITTS

Keep your face to the sunshine and you cannot see the shadow.

HELEN KELLER

There is very little difference in people, but that little difference makes a big difference. The little difference is attitude. The big difference is whether it is positive or negative.

W. CLEMENT STONE

It is not the situation. It is your reaction to the situation.

BOB CONKLIN

There are two big forces at work, external and internal. We have very little control over external forces such as tornadoes, earthquakes, floods, disasters, illness, and pain. What really matters is the internal force. How do I respond to those disasters? Over that I have complete control.

LEO BUSCAGLIA

If you will call your troubles experiences, and remember that every experience develops some latent force within you, you will grow vigorous and happy, however adverse your circumstances may seem to be.

JOHN MILLER

Diseases can be our spiritual flat tires—disruptions in our lives that seem to be disasters at the time but end by redirecting our lives in a meaningful way.

BERNIE SIEGEL

Out of difficulties grow miracles.

LA BRUYÉRE

Great emergencies and crises show us how much
greater our vital resources are than we had supposed.

WILLIAM JAMES

In the depth of winter I finally learned
that there was in me an invincible summer.

ALBERT CAMUS

God gave us our memories so that we might have roses in December.

J. M. BARRIE

I'm not afraid of storms for I'm learning how to sail my ship.

LOUISA MAY ALCOTT

Help us to be the always hopeful gardeners of the spirit who know that
without darkness nothing comes to birth as without light nothing flowers.

MAY SARTON

The quickest way to change your attitude toward pain
is to accept the fact that everything that happens to us
has been designed for our spiritual growth.

M. SCOTT PECK

When somebody is angry with us, we draw a halo around his or her head, in our minds. Does the person stop being angry then? Well, we don't know! We know, though, that when we draw a halo around a person, suddenly the person starts to look like an angel to us.

JOHN LENNON AND YOKO ONO

Picture yourself placing your problem inside a pale, yellow balloon, letting it go, watching it drift until it is a tiny pastel dot in the sky.

BARBARA MARKOFF

Whenever something good happens, write it down. Buy a special notebook . . . and use it to list all the good in your life.

PETER MCWILLIAMS AND JOHN-ROGER

It doesn't hurt to be optimistic. You can always cry later.

LUCIMAR SANTOS DE LIMA

The average pencil is seven inches long, with just a half-inch eraser—in case you thought optimism was dead.

ROBERT BRAULT

Pessimism never won any battle.

DWIGHT D. EISENHOWER

Stop the mindless wishing that things would be different. Rather than wasting time and emotional and spiritual energy in explaining why we don't have what we want, we can start to pursue other ways to get it.

GREG ANDERSON

Man is so made that whenever anything fires his soul, impossibilities vanish.

JEAN DE LA FONTAINE

Deep within man dwell those slumbering powers; powers that would astonish him, that he never dreamed of possessing; forces that would revolutionize his life if aroused and put into action.

ORISON S. MARDEN

Within you right now is the power to do things you never dreamed possible. This power becomes available to you just as soon as you can change your beliefs.

MAXWELL MALTZ

Exhilaration of life can be found only with an upward look. This is an exciting world. It is cram-packed with opportunity. Great moments wait around every corner.

RICHARD DEVOS

Enthusiasm is the greatest asset in the world. It beats money and power and influence.

HENRY CHESTER

Nothing splendid has ever been achieved except by those who dared
to believe that something inside of them was superior to circumstance.

BRUCE BARTON

It is the ultimate wisdom of the mountains that we are never
so much human as when we are striving for what is beyond our
grasp, and that there is no battle worth the winning save that
against our own ignorance and fear.

JAMES RAMSEY ULLMAN

I keep the telephone of my mind open to peace, harmony, health, love,
and abundance. Then whenever doubt, anxiety, or fear try to call me,
they keep getting a busy signal and soon they'll forget my number.

EDITH ARMSTRONG

You can do anything you wish to do, have anything
you wish to have, be anything you wish to be.

ROBERT COLLIER

People become really quite remarkable when they start
thinking that they can do things. When they believe
in themselves they have the first secret of success.

NORMAN VINCENT PEALE

What lies behind us and what lies before us
are small matter compared to what lies within us.

RALPH WALDO EMERSON

No matter what level of your ability, you have
more potential than you can ever develop in a lifetime.

JAMES MCCAY

Everyone has got it in him, if he will only make up his
mind and stick at it. None of us is born with a stop-valve on
his powers or with a set limit to his capacities. There is no
limit possible to the expansion of each one of us.

CHARLES SCHWAB

Everyone has inside of him a piece of good news. The good
news is that you don't know how great you can be! How much you
can love! What you can accomplish! And what your potential is!

ANNE FRANK

The power which resides in man is new in nature,
and none but he knows what that is which he can do,
nor does he until he has tried.

RALPH WALDO EMERSON

Ask, and it shall be given you; seek, and ye shall find;
knock, and it shall be opened unto you.
For every one that asketh, receiveth; and he that seeketh, findeth;
and to him that knocketh it shall be opened.

MATTHEW 7:7, 8

Trust yourself.
You know more than you think you do.

BENJAMIN SPOCK

If we did all the things we are capable of doing,
we would literally astound ourselves.

THOMAS ALVA EDISON

Each of us makes his own weather, determines the color of the skies
in the emotional universe which he inhabits.

BISHOP FULTON J. SHEEN

Every beauty and greatness in this world is created by a single
thought or emotion inside a man. Every thing we see today,
made by past generations, was, before its appearance, a thought
in the mind of a man or an impulse in the heart of a woman.

KAHLIL GIBRAN

Be brave enough to live creatively. The creative is the place where
no one else has ever been. You have to leave the city of your comfort
and go into the wilderness of your intuition. You cannot get there by
bus, only by hard work, risking and by not quite knowing what you
are doing. What you will discover will be wonderful: yourself.

ALAN ALDA

Be not afraid of life. Believe that life is worth living, and your belief will help create the fact.

WILLIAM JAMES

Your living is determined not so much by what life brings to you as by the attitude you bring to life.

JOHN MILLER

I am not discouraged, because every wrong attempt discarded is another step forward.

THOMAS ALVA EDISON

What is defeat? Nothing but education, nothing but the first step toward something better.

WENDELL PHILLIPS

To every disadvantage there is a corresponding advantage.

W. CLEMENT STONE

Look at everything as though you were seeing it either for the first or last time. Then your time on earth will be filled with glory.

BETTY SMITH

One for whom the pebble has value must be surrounded by treasures wherever he goes.

PAR LAGERKVIST

We're all only fragile threads, but what a tapestry we make.

JERRY ELLIS

Today, let's give thanks for life.
For life itself. For simply being born!

DAPHNE ROSE KINGMA

Spirituality

Faith

Prayer

God

Soul

When I use the word spirituality, I don't necessarily mean religion;
I mean whatever it is that helps you feel connected
to something that is larger than yourself.

DEAN ORNISH

The spiritual life does not remove us from the world
but leads us deeper into it.

HENRI J. M. NOUWEN

The fact that I can plant a seed and it becomes a flower, share
a bit of knowledge and it becomes another's, smile at someone
and receive a smile in return, are to me continual spiritual exercises.

LEO BUSCAGLIA

Faith is the evidence of things not seen.

1 HEBREWS 11:1

They understand but little who understand only what can be explained.

MARIE EBNER-ESCHENBACH

Some things have to be believed to be seen.

RALPH HODGSON

Faith is like electricity. You can't see it, but you can see the light.

ANONYMOUS

**Faith is the strength by which a shattered world
shall emerge into the light.**

HELEN KELLER

Live your beliefs and you can turn the world around.

HENRY DAVID THOREAU

**If you can't have faith in what is held up to you for faith,
you must find things to believe in yourself, for life
without faith in something is too narrow a space to live.**

GEORGE EDWARD WOODBERRY

I am one of those who would rather sink with faith than swim without it.

STANLEY BLADWIN

**If a blade of grass can grow in a concrete walk and a fig tree in the side
of a mountain cliff, a human being empowered with an invincible faith
can survive all odds the world can throw against his tortured soul.**

ROBERT H. SCHULLER

Faith is not knowledge of what the mystery of the universe is, but
the conviction that there is a mystery, and that it is greater than us.

RABBI DAVID WOLPE

Faith is our direct link to universal wisdom, reminding us
that we know more than we have heard or read or studied—
that we have only to look, listen, and trust the love and wisdom
of the Universal Spirit working through us all.

DAN MILLMAN

Believe in something larger than yourself.

BARBARA BUSH

Faith is knowing there is an ocean because you have seen a brook.

WILLIAM ARTHUR WARD

Faith is, above all, openness; an act of trust in the unknown.

ALAN WATTS

Faith is believing before receiving.

ALFRED A. MONTAPERT

Faith is not being sure where you're going but going anyway.

FREDRICK BUECHNER

Faith is to believe what we do not see;
the reward of this faith is to see what we believe.

Saint Augustine

You can do very little with faith, but you can do nothing without it.

Samuel Butler

All things are possible to him who believes.

Mark 9:23

Faith is the bird that feels the light
and sings when the dawn is still dark.

Rabindranath Tagore

Do not have your concert first and tune your
instruments afterwards. Begin the day with God.

James Hudson Taylor

All my life I have risen regularly at four o'clock and have gone into
the woods and talked to God. There He gives me my orders for the day.

George Washington Carver

The strength of a man consists in finding out the
way in which God is going, and going in that way too.

HENRY WARD BEECHER

God gives us always strength enough, and sense
enough, for everything He wants us to do.

JOHN RUSKIN

God gave burdens, also shoulders.

JEWISH SAYING

There is literally nothing that I ever asked to do,
that I asked the blessed Creator to help me
to do, that I have not been able to accomplish.

GEORGE WASHINGTON CARVER

Here on earth, God's work must surely be our own.

JOHN. F. KENNEDY

God can dream a bigger dream for you than you can dream
for yourself, and your role on Earth is to attach yourself
to that divine force and let yourself be released to it.

OPRAH WINFREY

We were born to make manifest the glory of God that is
within us. It's not just in some of us, it's in everyone.

NELSON MANDELA

I believe God is managing affairs and that He doesn't need
any advice from me. With God in charge, I believe
everything will work out for the best in the end.

HENRY FORD

In a world filled with causes for worry and anxiety . . . we need
the peace of God standing guard over our hearts and minds.

JERRY McCANT

Remember that everything has God's fingerprints on it.

RICHARD CARLSON

There is not a flower that opens, not a seed that falls
into the ground, and not an ear of wheat that nods on the end
of its stalk in the wind that does not preach and proclaim
the greatness and the mercy of God to the whole world.

THOMAS MERTON

Millions of angels are at God's command.

BILLY GRAHAM

The Holy Spirit . . . wants to flow through us and realize
all these wonderful possibilities in the world—if we only open
ourselves and allow it to happen.

BR. DAVID STEINDL-RAST

Do you not know that you are God's temple
and that God's spirit dwells within you?

1 CORINTHIANS 3:16

God does not ask your ability, or your inability.
He asks only your availability.

MARY KAY ASH

When you have succeeded in enshrining God
within your heart, you will see Him everywhere.

SWAMI SHIVANANDA

God dwells wherever man lets Him in.

JEWISH SAYING

God is love.

1 JOHN 4:8

God loves you. God doesn't want anyone to be hungry and oppressed. He
just puts his big arms around everybody and hugs them up against himself.

NORMAN VINCENT PEALE

God loves us the way we are but He
loves us too much to leave us that way.

LEIGHTON FORD

The best minister is the human heart; the best teacher is time;
the best book is the world; the best friend is God.

JEWISH SAYING

I love God, and when you get to know Him, you find He's a Livin' Doll.

JANE RUSSELL

I don't believe in God. Just try getting a plumber on the weekend.

WOODY ALLEN

God comes at last when we think he is farthest off.

JAMES HOWELL

God gave you a gift of 86,400 seconds today.
Have you used one to say "thank you"?

WILLIAM ARTHUR WARD

If you begin to live life looking for the God that is
all around you, every moment becomes a prayer.

FRANK BIANCO

A single grateful thought toward heaven is the most complete prayer.

GOTTHOLD EPHRAIM LESSING

Prayer may not change things for you,
but it for sure changes you for things.

SAMUEL SHOEMAKER

Get down on your knees and thank God you are on your feet.

IRISH SAYING

Time spent on the knees in prayer will do more to remedy
heart strain and nerve worry than anything else.

GEORGE DAVID STEWART

You pray in your distress and in your need; would that you might pray also in the fullness of your joy and in your days of abundance.

KAHLIL GIBRAN

I never went to bed in my life and I never ate a meal in my life without saying a prayer. I know my prayers have been answered thousands of times, and I know that I never said a prayer in my life without something good coming of it.

JACK DEMPSEY

God answers all our prayers. Sometimes the answer is yes. Sometimes the answer is no. Sometimes the answer is, you've got to be kidding!

JIMMY CARTER

Why is it when we talk to God we are said to be praying, and when God talks to us we're said to be schizophrenic?

LILY TOMLIN

A grandfather was walking through his yard when he heard his granddaughter repeating the alphabet in a tone of voice that sounded like a prayer. He asked her what she was doing. The little girl explained: "I'm praying, but I can't think of exactly the right words, so I'm just saying all the letters, and God will put them together for me, because He knows what I'm thinking."

CHARLES B. VAUGHAN

When you recover or discover something that nourishes your soul and brings joy, care enough about yourself to make room for it in your life.

JEAN SHINODA BOLEN

It's important to be heroic, ambitious, productive, efficient, creative, and progressive, but these qualities don't necessarily nurture the soul. The soul has different concerns, of equal value: downtime for reflection, conversation, and reverie; beauty that is captivating and pleasuring; relatedness to the environs and to people; and any animal's rhythm of rest and activity.

THOMAS MOORE

Excite the soul, and the weather and the town and your condition in the world all disappear; the world itself loses its solidity, nothing remains but the soul and the Divine Presence in which it lives.

RALPH WALDO EMERSON

The soul is awakened through service.

ERICA JONG

Souls are made of dawn-stuff and starshine.

ELBERT HUBBARD

I was thrown out of college for cheating on the metaphysics exam; I looked into the soul of the boy next to me.

WOODY ALLEN

Nobody grows old by merely living a number of years. People grow old only by deserting their ideals. Years wrinkle the face, but to give up enthusiasm wrinkles the soul.

WATTERSON LOWE

The purpose of life on earth is that the soul should grow— So Grow! By doing what is right.

ZELDA FITZGERALD

The soul . . . is audible, not visible.

HENRY WADSWORTH LONGFELLOW

Soul appears when we make room for it.

THOMAS MOORE

Wealth

True abundance is not about gathering more things, it's about
touching the place in us that is connected to the divine source of
abundance, so that we know what we need in the moment will be provided.

MARY MANIN MORRISSEY

It's time we put thoughts of lack behind us. It's time for us
to discover the secrets of the stars, to sail to an uncharted land,
to open up a new heaven where our spirits can soar.

SARAH BAN BREATHNACH

It is good to have things that money can buy, but it is also good to
check up once in awhile and be sure we have the things money can't buy.

GEORGE HORACE LORIMER

Ordinary riches can be stolen, real riches cannot. In your soul are
infinitely precious things that cannot be taken from you.

OSCAR WILDE

Let us not get so busy or live so fast that we can't listen to
the music of the meadow or the symphony that glorifies the forest.
Some things in the world are far more important than wealth;
one of them is the ability to enjoy simple things.

DALE CARNEGIE

It is wealth to be content.

LAO-TZU

Who is rich? He that rejoices in his portion.

BENJAMIN FRANKLIN

If you're happy, you're wealthy! Happiness doesn't need a bank account.

SR. MARY CHRISTELLE MACALUSO

**Wealth . . . is a relative thing since he that has little and wants
less is richer than he that has much but wants more.**

CHARLES CALEB COLTON

Sometimes when you have everything, you can't really tell what matters.

CHRISTINA ONASSIS

The only question with wealth is what you do with it.

JOHN D. ROCKEFELLER, JR.

**The rich man is not one who is in possession of much,
but one who gives much.**

SAINT JOHN CHRYSOSTOM

Having given all he had,
He then is very rich indeed.

LAO-TZU

If you see yourself as prosperous, you will be.
If you see yourself as continually hard up,
that is exactly what you will be.

ROBERT COLLIER

Prosperity is just around the corner.

HERBERT HOOVER

Wealth is not his that has it, but his who enjoys it.

BENJAMIN FRANKLIN

**Colors fade, temples crumble,
empires fall, but wise words endure.**

EDWARD THORNDIKE

INDEX

A

Atwood, Margaret 363
Augustine, Saint 349, 405
Aurelius, Marcus 165, 256
Austen, Jane 120
Austin, Emory 208
Ausubel, Kenny 325

B

Baal Shem, Israel 173
Baba, Meher 150
Bacall, Lauren 31
Bach, Richard 12, 100, 231, 245, 254
Bachelard, Gaston 318
Bacon, Ernst 297
Bacon, Francis 374
Baez, Joan 100, 164
Bagehot, Walter 120, 162
Bailey, Pearl 190, 366
Baker, George 254
Baker, Harrison 114
Baldwin, James 230
Ball, Lucille 2, 23
Ballantyne, Sheila 185
Bankhead, Tallulah 87
Bannister, Roger 187
Barber, Janette 44
Barfield, Jesse 234
Barrett, Rona 63
Barrie, James M. 75, 104, 146, 182,
    313, 340, 358, 392
Barry, Dave 242
Barrymore, Ethel 50

Barth, Karl 351
Barton, Bruce 21, 190, 257, 395
Battista, O. A. 121, 320
Baum, Vicki 63
Baxter, Anne 203
Beecher, Henry Ward 99, 135, 329, 384,
    406
Beerbohm, Max 134
Beltaire, Mark 373
Benchley, Robert 147, 210
Bennett, Arnold 317
Bennett, Dan 224
Bennett, William J. 264, 265
benShea, Noah 51
Berenson, Bernard 139, 173
Bereny, Gail Rubin 144
Berger, Arthur Asa 353
Bergman, Ingmar 318
Bergson, Henri 190, 308
Bering, Frank 214
Berle, Milton 43, 272
Bernhardt, Sarah 96
Berra, Yogi 153, 227
Berrigan, Daniel 218
Berry, John 226
Berry, Thomas 372
Betjeman, Sir John 115
Bettelheim, Bruno 76
Beudoin, Patricia C. 70
Beynon, Marie 197
Beyondananda, Swami 347
Bhaerman, Steve 347
Bianco, Frank 410

E

J

K

M

S

X

Xenophon 292

Y

Yeats, William Butler 55, 350
Young, Margaret 278
Yutang, Lin 102, 265

Z

Zadra, Dan 237
Ziglar, Zig 166
Zohar 104, 319
Zola, Emile 241
Zucker, David 136
Zukav, Gary 348
Zurtarti, Pesikta 16

ABOUT THE AUTHOR

Allen Klein is an award-winning professional speaker and best-selling author. He teaches people worldwide how to use humor to deal with not-so-funny stuff. In addition to this book, Klein is also author of Quotations to Cheer You Up, Up Words for Down Days, The Change-Your-Life Quote Book and The Lift-Your-Spirits Quote Book.

For more information about Klein or his presentations go to *www.allen klein.com,* E-mail him at *Author@allenklein.com* or write to him at 1034 Page Street, San Francisco, CA 94117.